MOON
AND
TURTLE

knitting
patterns
with
variations

POM POM PRESS

LONDON

Published in 2021 by Pom Pom Press
Text: ©Kiyomi Burgin & Sachiko Burgin
Photographs: ©Oliver James Brooks
Design: Oliver James Brooks
kshandknitdesign.com

ISBN: 978-1-9160295-6-9
A catalogue record for this book is available from the British Library.

Editors: Lydia Gluck + Meghan Fernandes
Managing Editor: Amy Collins
Publisher + Marketing Director: Belinda Johnson
**UK Wholesale Manager +
Community Liaison:** Sophie Heathscott
Features Editor: Francesca Baldry
**Production Coordinator + Retail
Manager:** Alice Sleight
Social Media + Digital Content Coordinator:
Sofia Aatkar
Studio Managers: Anoushka Haroutounian
+ Gayle Taliaferro Gilner
Copy Editor: Annie Prime
Consultant: Emi Ito
Technical Editor: Laura Chau + Jemima Bicknell
Models: Greg Moogk + Paul Tseng
Hair: Kazuo Mitamura
Greg's Temporary Tattoos: Designed by Miss Lee

Yarn Support: Akara Yarn, Briggs & Little, Green Mountain Spinnery, Peace Fleece, Qing Fibre, Viola

Sample Knitters: Emily Foden (Black Lewsky Hood + Bone / Bluefinch PokaPoka Hat), Stacey McDonald (Willow / Honey Bear Zener Socks), Svetlana Bogdanov (Grey Kordy Sweater + Spice Cesium Redux Cardigan)

Test Knitters: Abby Terranova, Alexandra Shcherbakova, Anja Daugbjerg Hansen, Anna Hirst, Annri Doi Vroom, Beate Nolte, Becky Joiner, Beth Leath, Cardner, Chantelle Martin, Eileen Mitchard, Erin Pyne, Fiona Boey, Injeong Kim, Irene Dieryck, Jade Kelley, Jaimie Noy, Kim Saenz, Kristi Visser, Kristina Russell, Maria (@conunpocodehilo), Marina Carboni, Mary Alice Kohs, Metta Karlsson, Paige Humecki, Rachel Offerdahl, Rebecca Newman, Sara McDermott, Sarah Fisher, Stacey McDonald, Susanne Wachter, Sylvan Tsai, Tatiana Volkova, Veronica Jackson, Victoria Salmon, Virpi Sipelaeinen

Non-Knit Wardrobe Pieces: Handsewn by Kiyomi and our mom, Gail Burgin, using fabric from Fabcycle Vancouver and Kallisti Quilts

Black canvas and yellow corduroy wide-leg trousers styled with *Kinsan, Ginsan, Kordy, Zener,* and *ESP - True Bias Lander Pants* with modifications

Light blue, dark blue, and dark green turtleneck tops styled with *PokaPoka - Kwik Sew 4069* with modifications

Pink top styled with *PokaPoka - French Navy Patterns Stellan Tee* with modifications

Pinstripe 'Samue' jacket* styled with *ESP -* #1 from *Japanese Casual Wear* (和のふだん着) with modifications

Black and white print Nani Iro blouse styled with *ESP -* #12 from *Shirt & Blouse by Yoshiko Tsukiori*

Navy, red, and yellow Asanoha (hemp leaf) print trousers styled with *Cesium Redux - Vogue Patterns 9139 view B*

Pale green onion dyed jacket styled with *Lewsky* and *Trionyx - McCall's 6613* with modifications

Black wrap 'Monpei' trousers* styled with *Lewsky* and *Trionyx - Folkwear 112 Japanese Field Clothing*

Pink and black gauze wrap dresses styled with *Trionyx* - improvised pattern

*The Japanese-inspired garments in this book were made and worn by people of Japanese heritage.

If you are interested in making these sewn garments, please consider whether or not it is appropriate for you to do so. We invite everyone to engage with questions and boundaries regarding cultural appropriation versus appreciation and how best to honour culturally rooted heritage makers.

Printed in the UK by Pureprint Group Limited, a CarbonNeutral® Company, on 100% recycled FSC® certified paper. Cover laminated with plastic-free biodegradable eco-film. Carbon Balanced with the World Land Trust.

For pattern corrections, please visit pompommag.com/errata

POM POM PRESS
Hackney Downs Studios,
Charcoal Hall
Amhurst Terrace
London
E8 2BT
United Kingdom
pompommag.com

To all twins who are collaborators or
competitors, who live closely or at
a great distance from each other, who
are best friends or have not spoken in
years, and to those who have lost their
twin or have never known them at all.
This book is dedicated to you both.

TABLE OF CONTENTS

0 6

Editors' Foreword

0 8

Authors' Introduction

1 0

Pattern Info

5 2

Zener

1 2

Kinsan

5 8

Cesium Redux

2 6

Ginsan

7 2

Kordy

3 6

PokaPoka

8 2

Lewsky

4 4

Trionyx

9 0

ESP

9 4

Twin Talk

9 6

Acknowledgements

9 7

Abbreviations

EDITORS' FOREWORD

Since the early days of our magazine, *Pom Pom Quarterly*, we have received design after beautiful design proposal from sisters Kiyomi and Sachiko Burgin. Each time a submission from one or both of them crossed our desks, we were astounded by the drawings, attention to detail, sense of style, and of course by the designs themselves. Though the proposals always conveyed the uniqueness of each twin, there was undoubtedly a resemblance among them, much like Ki and Chi themselves. Over the years, we've published eight of their designs collectively and, serendipitously, all but one of those were included in issues in which both of them were featured.

As the Burgins became a consistent part of the Pom Pom Publishing story, we realised how much potential there was for a collection that would appeal to legions of knitters and the people they love to knit for. The twins' style references are broad and fresh, reflecting the pace and atmosphere of their urban environment as well as a considered, minimalist approach that prioritises timelessness and quality construction alongside interesting making.

The versatility of the patterns in Moon & Turtle is remarkable- they're equally at home in your everyday life as at a special destination or event like a wedding (as you'll read later!). They are also distinguished by their ability to appeal to many people. Although the models in this book only represent a few body types and gender representations, we cannot wait to see these knits on myriad readers and look forward to sharing your projects on social media to showcase the many possibilities contained within these pages.

We are grateful to the Burgins for entrusting their vision for this book to us, while also running with and executing their ideas while the COVID-19 pandemic kept us from working together in person. The overall inclusive concept for the knitwear designs in *Moon & Turtle* is at the very heart of what we hope to publish at Pom Pom, and we are thrilled with the results of Ki and Chi's work on this magical volume.

Meghan Fernandes & Lydia Gluck
Austin & London, 2021

AUTHORS' INTRODUCTION

There are a few questions that we know other twins must get asked as much as we do. We hear them all the time: "Can you read each other's minds?", "Feel each other's pain?", "Do you ever play tricks on people?", "What's it like being a twin?"

In general, people seem very intrigued and curious about twins and are often keen to discover our similarities as well as our differences. As an identical twin, you are constantly being compared and contrasted with one another.

We were fortunate to grow up in a household that encouraged us to pursue our own interests, treating us each as individuals. Our mom rarely dressed us the same and was quick to correct people who wanted to treat us as the same person. Still, the need to prove our individuality was strong, and for many years we tried very hard not to appear like twins by adopting different styles of dress and hair. Today, looking different from one another is not really important to us, and we embrace our similarities, as well as our differences.

Although we each set out on our own journey, it's funny how our paths have once again converged with knitting and design.

We've always collaborated on projects ever since we were kids, colouring the same drawing, or building a paper-mâché project together. However we hadn't collaborated much on knitting in the past. Years ago, we tried to knit a sweater together, each taking on different pieces, such as the back, front, and sleeves, only to find that when we tried to sew it all together, the various pieces didn't fit! We discovered that we have completely different knitting gauges! Perhaps this was part of the reason we were always hesitant to work together on knitting.

But time passes and memories fade, and for the 30th issue of *Pom Pom*

Quarterly we had our first collaborative knitting design published. The design was called *Isobue*, and was a top-down raglan-style sweater, but knit in separate pieces that buttoned together for a mix-and-match approach. We found that we enjoyed working together on knit design and decided to pursue more collaborative projects. The result is *Moon and Turtle*.

With this collection, we tried to create a body of patterns that shows both of our unique styles. Admittedly, it wasn't easy and we didn't always agree, which perhaps is proof of how different we are. So, to meet each other halfway, we purposely kept all the designs very basic and simple, using classic shapes like raglans, yokes, and triangular shawls. Hopefully this will also ensure that these pieces remain timeless and wearable for as long as possible and for as many people as possible. Each design features a simple variation, so the knitter can tweak it to fit their taste, or to inspire them to take it one step further and add their own changes to the design.

We encourage you to be creative and make these designs your own - see them as a jumping-off point for making your own unique handknit creation that says YOU! Think about different embellishments, adding or subtracting certain details. Whatever you come up with is bound to be unique and special. We can't wait to see what you do with these patterns!

So why the title *Moon and Turtle*? If you've already flipped through the book, you will have noticed that it contains absolutely no knitting patterns relating to the moon or turtles! Sorry if that comes as a disappointment. Titles can be slightly misleading when you're not familiar with the context. So what is this *Moon and Turtle* thing all about?

You may be familiar with the English idiom 'like chalk and cheese', which is used to compare two things that look similar, but in actuality are nothing alike. The comparison of the moon and turtle has a similar meaning in Japan. *Tsuki to Suppon* / 月とスッポン (moon and soft-shelled turtle) is an idiom comparing the round shape of the moon to the roundness of the soft-shell turtle. Although they have the same shape, of course they are nothing alike. The moon is large, beautiful, and bright, and lives in the sky, whereas the small and endearingly unattractive *Suppon* prefers dark and murky dwellings in swampy water.

We liked this idiom a lot when we first heard it, as we felt it pretty much summed up how twins are often perceived - looking the same or similar physically, while still being individuals. This collection of designs follows a similar idea. A single design that when knit multiple times can look the same at first glance but, on closer observation, has small details that make it different.

PATTERN INFO

The designs in this book are intended to be worn by people of all genders. Garment patterns have been graded with nine sizes, equivalent to industry standards of sizes XS through 5XL, and to fit actual chest circumferences of 76 (86, 96, 106, 117, 127, 137, 147, 157)cm / 30 (34, 38, 42, 46, 50, 54, 58, 62)". Before beginning any pattern, please read over the pattern notes, and review the schematic for the full list of finished measurements.

To choose which pattern size to knit, first take the time to find your measurements or, if you can (and it's not a surprise gift), the measurements of the intended recipient. With a soft measuring tape, measure the circumference around the fullest part of your chest, then add / subtract the required amount of ease the pattern suggests, or the desired amount of ease you would like, and choose the closest pattern size. If you find you or your recipient is between sizes, you will have to decide whether you want more or less ease, and choose the size accordingly. Other key measurements to record and to help with size choice are the upper arm circumference, sleeve length from underarm to wrist, and body length from underarm to hem. Please refer to the pattern schematics for the finished measurements.

For the garments in this book, at least two different sleeve lengths and body lengths are given as standard* and tall**. Choose the length based on your measurements. If you fall between the lengths given, start by knitting the shortest length, and add additional length after shaping is completed. If you require more length than the longest length given, choose to work the longest length and add additional length by knitting extra rows after shaping is completed.

Please read over the pattern carefully before beginning. Since each pattern contains one or more variation options, mark the ones you plan to use beforehand to avoid confusion later. You might also notice that some patterns offer an 'Additional Variation Suggestion'. These are further variation ideas that are not written in the patterns, but are offered to give you ideas of how to alter the designs to your liking.

For best results, please be sure to wet block all finished pieces!

*approximate height of below 170cm / 5'7"
**approximate height of above 170cm / 5'7"

KINSAN

I'm really drawn to the 'mono' or coordinating outfits that are popular right now, but I struggle with wearing them since I always feel like I look like an M&M or a crayon. This set varies enough for me to feel comfortable wearing it. A classic striped raglan sweater is a great piece to have in any wardrobe. This design has a comfortable shaped neckline that won't ride up in the front. You can choose different sleeve and body length variations, as well as different stripe patterns to suit you. ~ *Kiyomi*

Honestly, I've always had a love-hate relationship with stripes. A bad memory from the early 2000s of pairing a striped sweater with a plaid shirt will forever be burned into my mind. But now, as a more self-aware adult with a mostly black and chromatone wardrobe, I appreciate how stripes can add a bit of colour and interest. I chose to knit my own *Kinsan* raglan with black as the main colour. Knitting with intensely deep colours can sometimes lead to a grand UFO (unfinished object!) fizzle out, what with all the eye strain and unnoticed stitch wrongdoings. To help the stockinette stitch progress and give myself something to look forward to, I chose a bright hunter orange paired with a neutral oatmeal. ~ *Sachiko*

Additional Variation Suggestion
There are probably a million different variations you could make of stripe patterns! If you'd like to see some additional examples, see page 25. If stripes are not your thing, feel free to knit this sweater in a single colour, or perhaps use a contrasting colour for only the sleeve cuffs and collar!

K
I
N
S
A
N

KINSAN

Sizes: 1 (2, 3, 4, 5, 6, 7, 8, 9)
Finished chest (fullest point) circumference:
86 (96.5, 106.5, 117, 127, 137, 147, 157.5, 167.5)
cm / 34 (38½, 42, 46, 50, 54, 58, 62, 66)" – to
be worn with up to 15cm / 6" positive ease

Greg's height is 173cm / 5'8", with a chest
(fullest point) circumference of 99cm / 39",
and is shown wearing the short sleeve tall
version in size 3 on pages 13 and 15.

Paul's height is 175cm / 5'9", with a chest (fullest point) circumference of 91.5cm / 36", and
is shown wearing the long sleeve tall version
in size 3 on pages 12 and 13.

Kiyomi's height is 155cm / 5'1", with a chest
(fullest point) circumference of 84cm / 33", and
is shown wearing the short sleeve
standard version in size 2 on pages 13 and 16.

Sachiko's height is 157.5cm / 5'2", with a
chest (fullest point) circumference of 76cm
/ 30", and is shown wearing the long sleeve
cropped version in size 1 on pages 13 and 14.

Yarn: Briggs & Little Sport (sport-weight;
100% wool; 393m / 430yds per 113g skein)

Shades Shown:
Stripe Pattern 1 – Tall body with long sleeves
Yarn A: Khaki
Yarn B: Sheeps Grey
Yarn C: Dark Grey

Stripe Pattern 2 – Standard body with
short sleeves
Yarn A: Natural White
Yarn B: Medium Grey
Yarn C: Fawn

Stripe Pattern 3 – Tall body with short sleeves
Yarn A: Navy Blue
Yarn B: Gold
Yarn C: Washed White

Stripe Pattern 4 – Cropped body with
long sleeves
Yarn A: Black
Yarn B: Hunter Orange
Yarn C: Sheeps Grey

Cropped Body
Short Sleeve
Yarn A: 1 (1, 1, 2, 2, 2, 2, 2, 2) skeins
Yarn B: 1 skein
Yarn C: 1 skein

OR
Yarn A: 285 (325, 365, 400, 455, 490, 535, 580, 635)
m / 310 (360, 400, 440, 500, 540, 590, 640, 700)yds
Yarn B: 75 (85, 95, 100, 110, 120, 135, 145, 160)
m / 85 (95, 100, 110, 120, 130, 145, 160, 175)yds
Yarn C: 45 (50, 55, 60, 65, 70, 80, 85, 95)m / 50
(55, 60, 65, 75, 80, 90, 95, 105)yds
Total yardage: 405 (460, 515, 560, 630, 680,
750, 810, 890)m / 445 (510, 560, 615, 695, 740,
825, 895, 980)yds

For Long Sleeve, an additional:
Yarn A: 45 (55, 55, 60, 60, 60, 65, 65, 60)m / 50
(60, 60, 65, 65, 65, 70, 70, 65)yds
Yarn B: 10 (15, 15, 25, 30, 30, 30, 35, 30)m / 15
(20, 20, 25, 35, 35, 35, 40, 35)yds
Yarn C: 15 (15, 20, 25, 30, 30, 30, 35, 35)m / 20
(20, 25, 30, 35, 35, 35, 40, 40)yds
Total yardage: 70 (85, 90, 110, 120, 120, 125,
135, 125)m / 85 (100, 105, 120, 135, 135, 140,
150, 140)yds

Standard Body
Short Sleeve
Yarn A: 2 (2, 2, 2, 2, 2, 3, 3, 3) skeins
Yarn B: 1 skein
Yarn C: 1 skein

OR
Yarn A: 420 (490, 550, 615, 695, 760, 835, 910,
990)m / 460 (535, 600, 675, 760, 830, 915, 995,
1085)yds
Yarn B: 105 (120, 140, 155, 175, 190, 210, 230,
250)m / 115 (135, 150, 170, 190, 210, 230, 250,
270)yds
Yarn C: 75 (90, 100, 110, 120, 130, 145, 155,
165)m / 85 (95, 105, 120, 135, 145, 155, 170,
185)yds
Total yardage: 600 (700, 790, 880, 990, 1080,
1190, 1295, 1405)m / 654 (763, 861, 959, 1079,
1177, 1297, 1412, 1531)yds

For Long Sleeve, an additional:
Yarn A: 100 (115, 120, 125, 140, 140, 150,
155, 160)m / 109 (125, 131, 136, 153, 153,
164, 169, 174)yds

Yarn B: 70 (80, 85, 95, 105, 110, 120, 125, 130) m / 76 (87, 93, 104, 114, 120, 131, 136, 142)yds
Yarn C: 15 (10, 10, 15, 20, 20, 20, 20, 25)m / 16 (11, 11, 16, 22, 22, 22, 22, 27)yds
Total yardage: 185 (205, 215, 235, 265, 270, 290, 300, 315)m / 202 (223, 234, 256, 289, 294, 316, 327, 343)yds

Tall Body
Short Sleeve
Yarn A: 2 (2, 2, 2, 3, 3, 3, 3, 3) skeins
Yarn B: 1 skein
Yarn C: 1 skein

OR
Yarn A: 500 (575, 640, 715, 795, 865, 945, 1025, 1115)m / 550 (630, 705, 785, 875, 950, 1040, 1130, 1225)yds
Yarn B: 130 (150, 165, 185, 210, 230, 250, 270, 295)m / 140 (160, 180, 200, 230, 250, 275, 300, 325)yds
Yarn C: 80 (85, 100, 110, 125, 135, 150, 165, 175)m / 85 (90, 110, 120, 135, 145, 165, 180, 190)yds
Total Yardage: 710 (810, 905, 1010, 1130, 1230, 1345, 1460, 1585)m / 775 (880, 995, 1105, 1240, 1345, 1480, 1610, 1740)yds

For Long Sleeve, an additional:
Yarn A: 115 (135, 145, 145, 165, 160, 170, 175, 175)m / 125 (150, 160, 160, 180, 175, 190, 195, 195)yds
Yarn B: 60 (70, 75, 80, 90, 90, 100, 110, 95)m / 65 (75, 80, 90, 100, 100, 110, 120, 105)yds
Yarn C: 15 (20, 20, 25, 25, 30, 30, 30, 35)m / 20 (25, 25, 30, 30, 35, 35, 35, 40)yds
Total yardage: 190 (225, 240, 250, 280, 280, 300, 315, 305)m / 210 (250, 265, 280, 310, 310, 335, 350, 340)yds

Additional Yardage for Contrasting Neckband:
Crew
Yarn B or C: 35 (35, 40, 40, 40, 45, 45, 50, 50)m / 40 (40, 45, 45, 45, 50, 50, 55, 55)yds
Mock
Yarn B or C: 75 (80, 80, 85, 85, 90, 95, 100, 110)m / 80 (85, 90, 90, 95, 100, 105, 115, 120)yds

Gauge: 22 sts & 30 rows = 10cm / 4" over St st on 3.5mm needles, after blocking.

Needles: 3.5mm / US 4 circular needles, 60-100cm / 24-40" length (depending on size worked) AND needles suitable for working small circumferences in the round. 3.25mm / US 3 circular needle, 60-100cm / 24-40" length (depending on size worked), 40cm / 16" length for neckband, AND needles suitable for working small circumferences in the round.
Note: Begin the yoke using needles suitable for working small circumferences in the round, then change to circular needles as the circumference increases.

Always use a needle size that will result in the correct gauge after blocking.

Notions: 4 stitch markers, stitch holders or waste yarn, tapestry needle

Notes: This pullover is worked in the round from the top down with raglan shaping. The back of the neck is shaped first by working back and forth, and then is joined in the round to create a shaped neckline. Different stripe patterns are given. Please choose the one you would like to use, or make your own. For stripe patterns with 4 rows or less between a colour change, loosely carry yarn down in back rather than breaking the yarn to help reduce the number of ends to weave in. It is also recommended to weave in ends as you go. Meterage / yardage will vary depending of stripe pattern. Different body lengths, sleeves lengths, and neck lengths are given. There is also an option of a contrasting colour neckband. Please read through pattern before beginning and choose the lengths you require / desire. It is recommended to choose a pattern size that gives you no more than 15cm / 6" of positive ease. Going with more ease might result in too much extra fabric at the underarms!

PATTERN BEGINS
Neck
Using larger circular needle, yarn A, and the Long-Tail Method, cast on 60 (62, 68, 70, 74, 78, 82, 88, 92) sts. Do not join in round.

Set-up row (WS): P1 for right front, PM, p12 (12, 14, 14, 16, 16, 16, 18, 18) for right sleeve, PM, p34 (36, 38, 40, 40, 44, 48, 50, 54) for back, PM, p12 (12, 14, 14, 16, 16, 16, 18, 18) for left sleeve, PM, p1 for left front.

Next row (RS)(inc): Kfb, SM, [k1, LLI, k to last st before marker, RLI, k1, SM] 3 times, kfb. *68 (70, 76, 78, 82, 86, 90, 96, 100) sts*

Next row (WS): Purl, slipping markers as you pass them.

Raglan inc row 1 (RS): [K to last st before marker, RLI, k1, SM, k1, LLI] 4 times. *8 sts inc*

Next row (WS): Purl.

Rep last 2 rows a further 2 times. *92 (94, 100, 102, 106, 110, 114, 120, 124) sts total; 20 (20, 22, 22, 24, 24, 24, 26, 26) sts for each sleeve, 42 (44, 46, 48, 48, 52, 56, 58, 62) sts for back, and 5 sts for each front*

Commence working the stripe pattern (pages 22 and 23), beg with row 1 of chart or written instructions and working through the rest of the pattern from this point forward, working last 2 rows a further 3 times. *116 (118, 124, 126, 130, 134, 138, 144, 148) sts total; 26 (26, 28, 28, 30, 30, 30, 32, 32) sts for each sleeve, 48 (50, 52, 54, 54, 58, 62, 64, 68) sts for back, and 8 sts for each front*

Raglan inc row 2 (RS): K1, M1L, [k to last st before marker, RLI, k1, SM, k1, LLI] 4 times, k to last st, M1R, k1. *10 sts inc*

Next row (WS): Purl.

Rep last 2 rows a further 3 times. *156 (158, 164, 166, 170, 174, 178, 184, 188) sts total; 34 (34, 36, 36, 38, 38, 38, 40, 40) sts for each sleeve, 56 (58, 60, 62, 62, 66, 70, 72, 76) sts for back, and 16 sts for each front*

Front Neck
Next row (RS)(inc): K1, M1L, [k to last st before marker, RLI, k1, SM, k1, LLI] 4 times, k to last st, M1R, k1, using Backwards-Loop Method cast on 2 (2, 3, 3, 3, 3, 3, 3, 3) sts. *10 sts inc, plus 2 (2, 3, 3, 3, 3, 3, 3, 3) cast-on sts at right front*

Next row (WS): P to end, using Backwards-Loop Method cast on 2 (2, 3, 3, 3, 3, 3, 3, 3) sts. *2 (2, 3, 3, 3, 3, 3, 3, 3) cast-on sts at left front*

Next row (RS)(inc): [K to last st before marker, RLI, k1, SM, k1, LLI] 4 times, using Backwards-Loop Method cast on 4 (4, 4, 4, 4, 5, 5, 5, 5) sts. *8 sts inc, plus 4 (4, 4, 4, 4, 5, 5, 5, 5) cast-on sts at right front*

Next row (WS): P to end, using Backwards-Loop Method cast on 4 (4, 4, 4, 4, 5, 5, 5, 5) sts. *186 (188, 196, 198, 202, 208, 212, 218, 222) sts total; 38 (38, 40, 40, 42, 42, 42, 44, 44) sts for each sleeve, 60 (62, 64, 66, 66, 70, 74, 76, 80) sts for back, and 25 (25, 26, 26, 26, 27, 27, 27, 27) sts for each front*

Join in round
Next row (RS): [K to last st before marker, RLI, k1, SM, k1, LLI] 4 times, using Backwards-Loop Method cast on 10 (12, 12, 14, 14, 16, 20, 22, 26) sts. Do not turn. Break yarn leaving a long tail, and one by one, slip sts on LH needle to RH needle past the next marker (front left shoulder marker) until you reach the marker at back left shoulder. This is now the beg of round. If necessary, change marker to a unique style. Rejoin yarn and knit 1 round to new beg of round marker to join work in the round, being careful not to twist. *204 (208, 216, 220, 224, 232, 240, 248, 256) sts total; 62 (64, 66, 68, 68, 72, 76, 78, 82) sts for front and back, 40 (40, 42, 42, 44, 44, 44, 46, 46) sts for each sleeve*

Raglan inc round A: [K1, LLI, k to last st before marker, RLI, k1, SM] 4 times. *8 sts inc*

Next round: Knit.

Rep last 2 rounds a further 11 (14, 15, 17, 18, 19, 21, 22, 23) times. *300 (328, 344, 364, 376, 392, 416, 432, 448) sts total; 86 (94, 98, 104, 106, 112, 120, 124, 130) sts for front and back, 64 (70, 74, 78, 82, 84, 88, 92, 94) sts for each sleeve*

Raglan inc round B: [K1, LLI, k to last st before marker, RLI, k1, SM, k across sleeve sts without increasing to next marker, SM] twice. *4 sts inc*

Next round: Knit.

Rep last 2 rounds a further 0 (0, 2, 3, 5, 6, 6, 8, 9) times. *304 (332, 356, 380, 400, 420, 444, 468, 488) sts total; 88 (96, 104, 112, 118, 126, 134, 142, 150) sts for front and back, 64 (70, 74, 78, 82, 84, 88, 92, 94) sts for each sleeve*

Divide for Body and Sleeves
Next round: K across back sts to next marker, remove marker (and all other markers as you come to them), slip next 64 (70, 74, 78, 82, 84, 88, 92, 94) sts to a holder or waste yarn for right sleeve, using the Backwards-Loop Method cast on 6 (10, 12, 14, 20, 22, 26, 28, 32) sts for underarm, k88 (96, 104, 112, 118, 126, 134, 142, 150) sts for front, slip 64 (70, 74, 78, 82, 84, 88, 92, 94) sts on to a holder or waste yarn for left sleeve, and using the Backwards-Loop Method, cast on 6 (10, 12, 14, 20, 22, 26, 28, 32) sts for underarm placing a marker in centre of sts for new beg of round, and rejoin for working in the round. *188 (212, 232, 252, 276, 296, 320, 340, 364) sts*

Body
Work even in St st in the round continuing to work stripe pattern until piece measures 21cm / 8½" from underarm for a cropped version, 29cm / 11½" for a standard length version, 34cm / 13½" for tall version, or until body measures 6cm / 2½" less than desired finished length.
Note: If a full stripe pattern rep cannot be worked by the time you reach desired length, continue working stripe in St st until complete, if desired.

Change to smaller circular needle and yarn A. Work in 2x2 Rib until hem measures 6cm / 2½". Cast off loosely in pattern.

SLEEVES
Return 64 (70, 74, 78, 82, 84, 88, 92, 94) held sleeve sts to larger needles.
Join yarn (keeping stripe pattern correct) at centre of underarm, pick up and knit 3 (5, 6, 7, 10, 11, 13, 14, 16) sts from cast-on, pick up and knit 1 st in gap between underarm and sleeve, k64 (70, 74, 78, 82, 84, 88, 92, 94) held sleeve sts, pick up and knit 1 st in the gap between underarm and sleeve, pick up and knit 3 (5, 6, 7, 10, 11, 13, 14, 16) sts along cast-on to centre of underarm. PM to indicate beg of round.

72 (82, 88, 94, 104, 108, 116, 122, 128) sts

Next round: K2 (4, 5, 6, 9, 10, 12, 13, 15), k2tog, k to last 4 (6, 7, 8, 11, 12, 14, 15, 17) sts, ssk, k to end. *70 (80, 86, 92, 102, 106, 114, 120, 126) sts*

Work sleeve by following instructions for *Short Sleeve, Long Sleeve Standard,* or for *Long Sleeve Tall.*

Short Sleeve ONLY
Work even in St st in the round continuing to work stripe pattern until sleeve measures 7.5cm / 3" from underarm, or 2.5cm / 1" less than desired finished length. If a full stripe pattern rep cannot be worked by the time you reach desired length, continue working stripe in St st until complete, if desired.

Change to yarn A.
Dec round: Dec 2 (0, 2, 0, 2, 2, 2, 0, 2) sts evenly over round. *68 (80, 84, 92, 100, 104, 112, 120, 124) sts*

Work in 2x2 Rib for 2.5cm / 1". Cast off in pattern.

Long Sleeve Standard ONLY
Work 13 (8, 6, 6, 4, 4, 3, 3, 3) rounds even in St st continuing to work stripe pattern.
Dec round: K1, k2tog, k to last 3 sts, ssk, k1. *2 sts dec*
Rep Dec round every following 14th (9th, 7th, 7th, 5th, 5th, 4th, 4th, 4th) round a further 7 (11, 14, 15, 20, 20, 23, 25, 26) times. *54 (56, 56, 60, 60, 64, 66, 68, 72) sts*

Work even in St st continuing to work stripe pattern until sleeve measures 38cm / 15" from underarm, or until sleeve measures 6cm / 2½" less than finished desired length.

Long Sleeve Tall ONLY
Work 15 (10, 8, 7, 5, 5, 4, 4, 4) rounds even in St st continuing to work stripe pattern.
Dec round: K1, k2tog, k to last 3 sts, ssk, k1. *2 sts dec*
Rep Dec round every following 16th (11th, 9th, 8th, 6th, 6th, 5th, 5th, 5th) round a further 7 (11, 14, 15, 20, 20, 23, 25, 26) times. *54 (56, 56, 60, 60, 64, 66, 68, 72) sts*

Work even in St st continuing to work stripe pattern until sleeve measures 46cm / 18" from underarm, or until sleeve measures 6cm / 2½" less than finished desired length.

Long Sleeve Cuff
Change to smaller needles and yarn A.

Dec round: [K7 (5, 12, 13, 13, 6, 9, 15, 7), k2tog] to end. *48 (48, 52, 56, 56, 56, 60, 64, 64) sts*
Work in 2x2 Rib until cuff measures 6cm / 2½". Cast off in pattern.

Neck Band
With RS facing, yarn A (or B or C for contrasting neckband), shorter circular needle and beg at back of left sleeve, pick up and knit 12 (12, 14, 14, 16, 16, 16, 18, 18) sts along top of left sleeve, 16 sts down curve of left neck to the centre cast-on sts, 22 (24, 26, 28, 28, 32, 36, 38, 42) sts along front of neck, 16 sts up curve of right neck, 12 (12, 14, 14, 16, 16, 16, 18, 18) sts along top of right sleeve, and 34 (36, 38, 40, 40, 44, 48, 50, 54) sts across back. Join to work in the round and PM to indicate beg of round. *112 (116, 124, 128, 132, 140, 148, 156, 164) sts*

Crew Neck ONLY
Work in 2x2 Rib for 3cm / 1¼". Cast off loosely in pattern.

Mock Neck ONLY
Work in 2x2 Rib for 11cm / 4½". Fold neck in half to WS, bringing needle parallel to inner neck edge.

Using LH needle tip, pick up the st closest to base of neck that corresponds with the first on LH needle, and keep this st on the LH needle tip. Knit this st together with next st on LH needle.
Rep last step once more, then cast off 1 st loosely.
Rep last 2 steps as set around neck until all sts have been bound off and neckband is folded down to inside around neck opening.
Break yarn and fasten off.

FINISHING
Weave in ends and block to measurements.

Stripe Patterns:
Stripe Pattern 1
Rows / Rounds 1-2: Work in St st using yarn A.
Rows / Rounds 3-6: Work in St st using yarn B.
Rows / Rounds 7-8: Work in St st using yarn C
Rows / Rounds 9-12: Work in St st using yarn B.
Rows / Rounds 13-24: Work in St st using yarn A.
Rows / Rounds 25-26: Work in St st using yarn C.
Rows / Rounds 27-36: Work in St st using yarn A.
Rep rows / rounds 1-36 for pattern.

Stripe Pattern 2
Rows / Rounds 1-4: Work in St st using yarn A.
Rows / Rounds 5-6: Work in St st using yarn B.
Rows / Rounds 7-8: Work in St st using yarn C
Rows / Rounds 9-10: Work in St st using yarn B.
Rows / Rounds 11-22: Work in St st using yarn A.
Rows / Rounds 23-28: As rows / rounds 5-10.
Rows / Rounds 29-36: Work in St st using yarn A.
Rep rows / rounds 1-36 for pattern.

Stripe Pattern 3
Rows / Rounds 1-4: Work in St st using yarn A.
Rows / Rounds 5-6: Work in St st using yarn B.
Rows / Rounds 7-8: Work in St st using yarn A.
Rows / Rounds 9-10: Work in St st using yarn C.
Rows / Rounds 11-12: Work in St st using yarn A.
Rows / Rounds 13-14: Work in St st using yarn B.
Rows / Rounds 15-22: Work in St st using yarn A.
Rows / Rounds 23-32: As rows / rounds 5-14.
Rows / Rounds 33-36: Work in St st using yarn A.
Rep rows / rounds 1-36 for pattern.

Stripe Pattern 4
Rows / Rounds 1-6: Work in St st using yarn A.
Rows / Rounds 7-8: Work in St st using yarn C.
Rows / Rounds 9-10: Work in St st using yarn B.
Rows / Rounds 11-24: Work in St st using yarn A.
Rows / Rounds 25-28: As rows / rounds 7-10.
Rows / Rounds 29-36: Work in St st using yarn A.
Rep rows / rounds 1-36 for pattern.

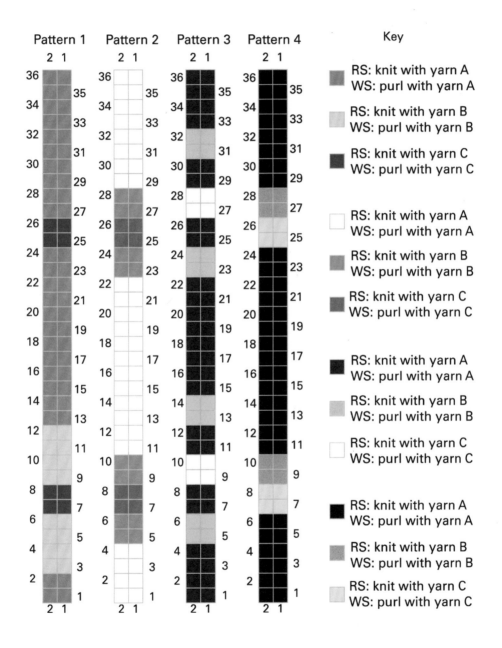

Pattern 1 Pattern 2 Pattern 3 Pattern 4

Key

RS: knit with yarn A
WS: purl with yarn A

RS: knit with yarn B
WS: purl with yarn B

RS: knit with yarn C
WS: purl with yarn C

RS: knit with yarn A
WS: purl with yarn A

RS: knit with yarn B
WS: purl with yarn B

RS: knit with yarn C
WS: purl with yarn C

RS: knit with yarn A
WS: purl with yarn A

RS: knit with yarn B
WS: purl with yarn B

RS: knit with yarn C
WS: purl with yarn C

RS: knit with yarn A
WS: purl with yarn A

RS: knit with yarn B
WS: purl with yarn B

RS: knit with yarn C
WS: purl with yarn C

Here are some additional stripe patterns and colour options to inspire you! Swatches are knit in Briggs & Little Sport.

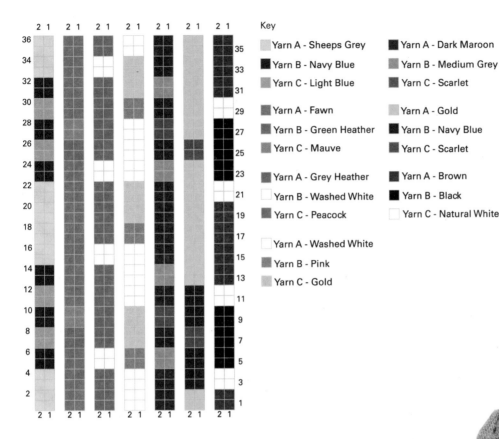

Key

Yarn A - Sheeps Grey	Yarn A - Dark Maroon
Yarn B - Navy Blue	Yarn B - Medium Grey
Yarn C - Light Blue	Yarn C - Scarlet
Yarn A - Fawn	Yarn A - Gold
Yarn B - Green Heather	Yarn B - Navy Blue
Yarn C - Mauve	Yarn C - Scarlet
Yarn A - Grey Heather	Yarn A - Brown
Yarn B - Washed White	Yarn B - Black
Yarn C - Peacock	Yarn C - Natural White
Yarn A - Washed White	
Yarn B - Pink	
Yarn C - Gold	

Schematic Measurements
a. Finished chest (fullest point) circumference: 86 (96.5, 106.5, 117, 127, 137, 147, 157.5, 167.5) cm / 34 (38½, 42, 46, 50, 54, 58, 62, 66)"
b. Length to underarm, cropped: 28cm / 11"
Length to underarm, standard: 35.5cm / 14"
Length to underarm, tall: 40.5cm / 16"
c. Upper arm circumference: 32.5 (37, 40, 42.5, 47, 49, 52.5, 55.5, 58)cm / 12¾ (14½, 15½, 16¾, 18½, 19¼, 20¾, 21¾, 23)"
d. Sleeve length, short: 10cm / 4"
e. Sleeve length, standard: 43cm / 17"
Sleeve length, tall: 51cm / 20"
f. Raglan depth: 21 (21, 22.5, 22.5, 24, 24.5, 25.5, 27.5, 28.5)cm / 7¼ (8, 8¾, 9½, 10½, 11, 11½, 12¼, 12¾)"
g. Back neck width: 16 (16.5, 17.5, 18.5, 18.5, 20, 22, 23, 25)cm / 6 (6½, 7, 7¼, 7¼, 8, 8¾, 9, 9¾)"

GINSAN

Kin Narita
and Gin Kanie
(known as
Kinsan Ginsan)
from Nagoya,
Japan were
the oldest
living twins
ever recorded.
They both lived
healthy lives
to the ages of
107 and 108,
respectively.
In Japanese,
kin means
gold, and *gin*
means silver.

Sort of a cardigan, kind of a jacket, this piece was designed to be roomy and big! Double knitting is utilised in the sleeve cuffs and neck edging to create extra cosiness with minimal bulk. The folded-style pockets are constructed without any seams. Actually, this whole piece is worked completely without seams!

Ginsan is designed to coordinate with the *Kinsan* raglan to make a twinset; every twin-themed knitting book obviously needs a twinset! Generally twinsets are a two-piece ensemble layered together. We wanted to create our twinset as two contemporary pieces that could be worn together or separately but weren't too 'matchy matchy'. Wearing a cardigan on top of a sweater might seem like too much to some, but if you live in a colder climate, or are always chilly (like us), you'll find this ensemble super cosy!

We think you'll find some interesting and surprising techniques and shaping in this deceivingly basic-looking design. There's a photo tutorial on our website as well to help with the pocket construction. We hope you'll learn something new!

Additional Variation Suggestion
The stripe detailing on the cuffs and neck
band coordinate with the *Kinsan* raglan,
but, of course, are optional. Knitting the
neckband in a completely contrasting
colour could look great too!

GINSAN

Sizes: 1 (2, 3, 4, 5, 6, 7, 8, 9)
Finished chest (fullest point) circumference, including bands: 102 (112, 122, 131, 141, 149, 159, 168, 178)cm / 40 (44, 48, 51½, 55½, 58½, 62½, 66, 70)" – to be worn with approx 20-25cm / 8-10" positive ease

Paul's height is 175cm / 5'9", with a chest (fullest point) circumference of 91.5cm / 36", and is shown wearing the tall sleeve version in size 5 on pages 27 and 35.

Kiyomi's height is 155cm / 5'1", with a chest (fullest point) circumference of 84cm / 33", and is shown wearing the standard sleeve version in size 2 on pages 26, 27 and 33.

Yarn: Briggs & Little Heritage (aran-weight; 100% wool; 197m / 215yds per 113g skein)

Yarn A, standard: 5 (6, 6, 7, 8, 8, 9, 9, 10) skeins
Yarn A, tall: 5 (6, 7, 7, 8, 9, 10, 10, 11) skeins
Yarn B (optional): 1 skein
Yarn C (optional): 1 skein

OR

Yarn A: approx. 870 (1000, 1125, 1205, 1390, 1505, 1635, 1745, 1915)m / 950 (1090, 1230, 1315, 1520, 1640, 1785, 1900, 2090)yds of aran-weight yarn
Yarn B (optional): approx. 30 (30, 35, 35, 40, 40, 45, 45, 45)m / 35 (35, 40, 40, 45, 45, 50, 50, 50)yds of aran-weight yarn
Yarn C (optional): approx. 30 (30, 35, 35, 40, 40, 45, 45, 45)m / 35 (35, 40, 40, 45, 45, 50, 50, 50)yds of aran-weight yarn

For tall sleeves, an additional: 90 (100, 115, 115, 125, 130, 145, 145, 160)m / 99 (110, 126, 126, 137, 142, 159, 159, 175)yds of yarn A.

Shades Shown:
Standard version (grey)
Yarn A: Medium Grey
Yarn B: Natural White
Yarn C: Fawn

Tall version (sheeps grey)
Yarn A: Sheeps Grey

Yarn B: Dark Grey
Yarn C: Natural White

Gauge: 16 sts & 23 rows = 10cm / 4" over St st on 5mm needles, after blocking.

30 sts & 52 rows = 10cm / 4" over double knit pattern on 3.75mm needles, after blocking.

Needles: 5mm / US 8 circular needle, 100cm / 40" length AND needles suitable for working small circumferences in the round, plus a spare needle for pockets and Three-Needle Cast-Off
4mm / US 6 circular needle, 100cm / 40" length, AND needles suitable for working small circumferences in the round, plus a spare circular needle for grafting
3.75mm / US 5 circular needle, 100cm / 40" length, plus a spare circular needle for grafting

Always use a needle size that will result in the correct gauge after blocking.

Notions: 4 stitch markers, 2 removable locking stitch markers, stitch holders or waste yarn, five 20-25mm / ¾-1" buttons (optional), tapestry needle

Notes: This oversized cardigan jacket is worked seamlessly from the top down in one piece. Stitches are cast on for the neck and the yoke is shaped in the raglan style. Stitches are then divided to work the body with pockets to hem. Sleeves are worked afterwards in the round and are finished with a double knit cuff with an optional stripe detail. The front band is worked in three parts; first, stitches are picked up around the upper body and neck and are worked in double knit with an optional stripe detail. The lower fronts are picked up and knit afterwards in rib with the option of working buttonholes. Finally, the pocket bags are worked at the end in the round and are finished with a Three-Needle Cast-Off. This cardigan was designed to be worn with approximately 20-25cm / 8-10" positive ease, however it can also be worn with less ease for a more fitted look, or with a greater amount of ease for a generous oversized fit.

PATTERN BEGINS
Neck
Using 5mm circular needle, yarn A, and the Long-Tail Method, cast on 60 (62, 62, 64, 70, 72, 72, 74, 76) sts.

Set-up row (WS): P3 for right front, PM, p14 (14, 14, 14, 16, 16, 16, 16, 16) for right sleeve, PM, p26 (28, 28, 30, 32, 34, 34, 36, 38) for back, PM, p14 (14, 14, 14, 16, 16, 16, 16, 16) for left sleeve, PM, p3 for left front.
Next row (RS): Knit, slipping markers as you pass them.

Shape Shoulders
Row 1 (WS)(inc): [P to last 2 sts before marker, RLIP, p2, SM, purl sleeve sts without increasing to next marker, SM, p2, LLIP] twice, p to end. *4 sts inc*
Row 2 (RS)(inc): [K to last 2 sts before marker, RLI, k2, SM, knit sleeve sts without increasing to next marker, SM, k2, LLI] twice, k to end. *4 sts inc*
Rep rows 1-2 a further 2 (2, 2, 3, 3, 3, 3, 4, 4) times. *84 (86, 86, 96, 102, 104, 104, 114, 116) sts total; 9 (9, 9, 11, 11, 11, 11, 13, 13) sts for each front, 14 (14, 14, 14, 16, 16, 16, 16, 16) sts for each sleeve, 38 (40, 40, 46, 48, 50, 50, 56, 58) sts for back*

Next row (WS): Purl.
Next row (RS)(inc): [K to last 2 sts before marker, RLI, k2, SM, k2, LLI] 4 times, k to end. *8 sts inc*
Next row (WS): Purl.
Rep last 2 rows a further 5 (5, 7, 7, 7, 9, 11, 12, 12) times. *132 (134, 150, 160, 166, 184, 200, 218, 220) sts total; 15 (15, 17, 19, 19, 21, 23, 26, 26) sts for each front, 26 (26, 30, 30, 32, 36, 40, 42, 42) sts for each sleeve, 50 (52, 56, 62, 64, 70, 74, 82, 84) sts for back*

Begin Raglan Shaping
Row 1 (RS): Knit.
Row 2 (WS): Purl.
Row 3 (RS): K1, M1L, [k to last 2 sts before marker, RLI, k2, SM, k2, LLI] 4 times, k to last st, M1R, k1. *10 sts inc*
Row 4 (WS): Purl.
Row 5 (RS): Knit.
Row 6 (WS): Purl.

Row 7 (RS): [K to last 2 sts before marker, RLI, k2, SM, k2, LLI] 4 times, k to end. *8 sts inc*
Row 8 (WS): Purl.
Rep rows 1-8 a further 3 (4, 4, 4, 5, 4, 4, 4, 5) times. *204 (224, 240, 250, 274, 274, 290, 308, 328) sts total; 27 (30, 32, 34, 37, 36, 38, 41, 44) sts for each front, 42 (46, 50, 50, 56, 56, 60, 62, 66) sts for each sleeve, 66 (72, 76, 82, 88, 90, 94, 102, 108) sts for back*

Rep rows 1-4 a further 2 (2, 2, 2, 2, 4, 4, 4, 4) times. *224 (244, 260, 270, 294, 314, 330, 348, 368) sts total; 31 (34, 36, 38, 41, 44, 46, 49, 52) sts for each front, 46 (50, 54, 54, 60, 64, 68, 70, 74) sts for each sleeve, 70 (76, 80, 86, 92, 98, 102, 110, 116) sts for back*

Place a removable marker into the last increase at the edge of each front. This will be used as a vantage point later on.

Divide for Body and Sleeves
Next row (RS): K31 (34, 36, 38, 41, 44, 46, 49, 52) left front sts to marker, remove marker (and all further markers as you pass them), place 46 (50, 54, 54, 60, 64, 68, 70, 74) left sleeve sts on waste yarn, using the Backwards-Loop Method cast on 6 (8, 12, 14, 16, 16, 20, 20, 22) sts, k70 (76, 80, 86, 92, 98, 102, 110, 116) back sts, place 46 (50, 54, 54, 60, 64, 68, 70, 74) right sleeve sts on waste yarn, using the Backwards-Loop Method cast on 6 (8, 12, 14, 16, 16, 20, 20, 22) sts, k31 (34, 36, 38, 41, 44, 46, 49, 52) right front sts to end. *144 (160, 176, 190, 206, 218, 234, 248, 264) sts*

Work even in St st back and forth for 4 (4, 4, 4, 5, 5, 5, 5, 5)cm / 1½ (1½, 1½, 1½, 2, 2, 2, 2, 2)", ending with a WS row.

Divide for Pockets
Next row (RS): Knit to 7 (8, 10, 12, 12, 15, 16, 18, 20) sts from end and turn, placing last 7 (8, 10, 12, 12, 15, 16, 18, 20) sts of row on holder or waste yarn.
Next row (WS): Purl to 7 (8, 10, 12, 12, 15, 16, 18, 20) sts from end and turn, placing last 7 (8, 10, 12, 12, 15, 16, 18, 20) sts of row on holder or waste yarn. *130 (144, 156, 166, 182, 188, 202, 212, 224) sts on needle*

Work over centre 130 (144, 156, 166, 182, 188, 202, 212, 224) sts until piece measures 16.5. (16.5, 16.5, 16.5, 18, 18, 18, 18, 18)cm / 6½ (6½, 6½, 6½, 7, 7, 7, 7, 7)" from sts on hold, ending with a WS row.

Next row (RS): K26 (26, 26, 26, 28, 28, 28, 28, 28) and place these sts on a holder or waste yarn, knit to end, and place last 26 (26, 26, 26, 28, 28, 28, 28, 28) sts of row on a holder or waste yarn. Place rem 78 (92, 104, 114, 126, 132, 146, 156, 168) sts onto a spare circular needle or separate piece of waste yarn. Break yarn.

Left Pocket Flap
With RS facing, place 7 (8, 10, 12, 12, 15, 16, 18, 20) sts on hold at left front edge onto 5mm circular needle and rejoin yarn A.
Next row (RS): K7 (8, 10, 12, 12, 15, 16, 18, 20), then pick up and knit 26 (26, 26, 26, 28, 28, 28, 28, 28) sts (approx 3 sts for every 4 rows) along the vertical side edge of centre panel to corner. *33 (34, 36, 38, 40, 43, 44, 46, 48) sts*

Work even in St st until pocket flap measures 16.5 (16.5, 16.5, 16.5, 18, 18, 18, 18, 18)cm / 6½ (6½, 6½, 6½, 7, 7, 7, 7, 7)" ending with a WS row. Break yarn and place sts on holder.

Right Pocket Flap
With RS facing, using 5mm circular needle and beg at corner of centre panel at the right front, rejoin yarn A.
Next row (RS): Pick up and knit 26 (26, 26, 26, 28, 28, 28, 28, 28) sts (approx 3 sts for every 4 rows) down along the vertical side edge of centre panel, place 7 (8, 10, 12, 12, 15, 16, 18, 20) sts on hold at right front edge onto needle, k7 (8, 10, 12, 12, 15, 16, 18, 20). *33 (34, 36, 38, 40, 43, 44, 46, 48) sts*

Work even in St st until pocket flap measures 16.5 (16.5, 16.5, 16.5, 18, 18, 18, 18, 18)cm / 6½ (6½, 6½, 6½, 7, 7, 7, 7, 7)", ending with a RS row.

Next row (WS): P33 (34, 36, 38, 40, 43, 44, 46, 48) sts for pocket flap, place 78 (92, 104, 114, 126, 132, 146, 156, 168) held centre panel sts onto working needle and purl across, place 33 (34, 36, 38, 40, 43, 44, 46, 48) held left pocket flap sts onto needle and purl to end.

Right pocket, centre panel, and left pocket are now joined; 144 (160, 176, 190, 206, 218, 234, 248, 264) sts
Note: The remainder of the pockets will be completed in a later step.

Work even in St st until piece measures 30.5 (30.5, 30.5, 30.5, 33, 33, 33, 33, 33)cm / 12 (12, 12, 12, 13, 13, 13, 13, 13)" from underarm, ending with a WS row, decreasing 0 (0, 0, 2, 2, 2, 2, 0, 0) sts evenly spaced along last row. *144 (160, 176, 188, 204, 216, 232, 248, 264) sts*

Hem
Change to 4mm circular needles.
Row 1 (RS): K3, [p2, k2] to last 5 sts, p2, k3.
Row 2 (WS): P3, [k2, p2] to last 5 sts, k2, p3.
Rep rows 1-2 until hem measures 7.5cm / 3".
Cast off loosely in patt.

SLEEVES
Return 46 (50, 54, 54, 60, 64, 68, 70, 74) sleeve sts to 5mm needles for working small circumferences.
Join yarn A at centre of underarm, pick up and knit 3 (4, 6, 7, 8, 8, 10, 10, 11) sts from cast-on, pick up and knit 2 (2, 2, 2, 1, 1, 1, 1, 1) sts in gap between underarm and sleeve, k46 (50, 54, 54, 60, 64, 68, 70, 74) sleeve sts, pick up and knit 2 (2, 2, 2, 1, 1, 1, 1, 1) sts in gap, pick up and knit 3 (4, 6, 7, 8, 8, 10, 10, 11) sts from cast-on to centre of underarm. PM to indicate beg of round. *56 (62, 70, 72, 78, 82, 90, 92, 98) sts*

Next round: K2 (3, 5, 6, 7, 7, 9, 9, 10), k2tog, k to last 4 (5, 7, 8, 9, 9, 11, 11, 12) sts, ssk, k to end. *54 (60, 68, 70, 76, 80, 88, 90, 96) sts*

Follow instructions for *Standard Sleeve* or *Tall Sleeve.*

Standard Sleeve ONLY
Work 20 (11, 6, 6, 5, 5, 3, 3, 2) rnds even in St st.
Dec round: K1, k2tog, k to last 3 sts, ssk, k1.
2 sts dec
Rep Dec round every following 21st (12th, 7th, 7th, 6th, 6th, 4th, 4th, 3rd) round a further 2 (4, 7, 7, 8, 9, 12, 12, 15) times.
48 (50, 52, 54, 58, 60, 62, 64, 64) sts

Work even in St st until sleeve measures 28cm / 11" from underarm, or until sleeve measures 5cm / 2" less than desired finished length.

Tall Sleeve ONLY
Work 29 (17, 10, 10, 8, 7, 5, 5, 4) rounds even in St st.
Dec round: K1, k2tog, k to last 3 sts, ssk, k1.
2 sts dec
Rep Dec round every following 30th (18th, 11th, 11th, 9th, 8th, 6th, 6th, 5th) round a further 2 (4, 7, 7, 8, 9, 12, 12, 15) times.
48 (50, 52, 54, 58, 60, 62, 64, 64) sts

Work even in St st until sleeve measures 40.5cm / 16" from underarm, or until sleeve measures 5cm / 2" less than desired finished length.

BOTH Styles
Change to 4mm needles. Cuff is worked in double knit.
Work *Solid Cuff* or *Striped Cuff*.

Solid Cuff
Round 1: [K1, sl1 pwise wyif] to end.
Round 2: [Sl1 pwise wyib, p1] to end.
Rep rounds 1-2 a further 11 times.
Continue to *Graft Cuff Edge*.

Striped Cuff
Round 1: [K1, sl1 pwise wyif] to end.
Round 2: [Sl1 pwise wyib, p1] to end.
Rounds 3-8: Rep rounds 1-2 a further 3 times.
Round 9: With yarn B, work round 1.
Round 10: With yarn A, work round 2.
Rounds 11-12: Rep rounds 9-10 once more.
Round 13: With yarn C, work round 1.
Round 14: With yarn A, work round 2.
Rounds 15-16: Rep rounds 13-14 once more.
Round 17: With yarn B, work round 1.
Round 18: With yarn A, work round 2.
Rounds 19-20: Rep rounds 17-18 once more.
Break yarns B and C.
With yarn A, rep rounds 1-2 a further 5 times.

Graft Cuff Edge
Next round: Slipping each st pwise, slip the knit sts onto the working needle and the purl sts onto a spare circular needle, held at the back.

24 (25, 26, 27, 29, 30, 31, 32, 32) sts on each needle that are held parallel to each other

Break yarn, leaving a tail that is approx 4 times the circumference of cuff. Thread tail onto a tapestry needle and graft front sts together with back sts.

Neckband
With 3.75mm circular needle, yarn A, and beg 2 rows below the removable marker that was placed in the last increase at right front edge, pick up and knit 36 (41, 43, 44, 48, 48, 50, 52, 57) sts (approx 3 sts for every 5 rows) up right front, then pick up and knit 50 (52, 52, 54, 60, 62, 62, 64, 66) sts along cast-on edge, then pick up and knit 36 (41, 43, 44, 48, 48, 50, 52, 57) sts down left front to 2 rows below the removable marker that was placed in the last increase at left front edge. Remove both removable markers. *122 (134, 138, 142, 156, 158, 162, 168, 180) sts*

Next row (WS): [K1tbl, yo] to last st, k1tbl. *243 (267, 275, 283, 311, 315, 323, 335, 359) sts*
Row 1 (RS): [Sl1 pwise wyif, k1] to last st, sl1 pwise wyif.
Row 2 (WS): [K1, sl1 pwise wyif] to last st, k1.
Rows 3-6: Rep rows 1-2 a further 2 times.

Solid Neckband ONLY
Work rows 1-2 a further 10 times in yarn A only, then continue to *Graft Neck Edge*.

Striped Neckband ONLY
Rows 7-8: With yarn B, work rows 1-2.
Rows 9-10: Rep rows 7-8 once more.
Rows 11-12: With yarn C, work rows 1-2.
Rows 13-14: Rep rows 11-12 once more.
Rows 15-16: With yarn B, work rows 1-2.
Rows 17-18: Rep rows 15-16 once more.
Break yarns B and C.
With yarn A, work rows 1-2 a further 4 times.

Graft Neck Edge
Slipping each st pwise, slip the knit sts onto the working needle and the purl sts onto a spare circular needle, held at the back.

GINSANN

121 (133, 137, 141, 155, 157, 161, 167, 179) sts on working needle, and 122 (134, 138, 142, 156, 158, 162, 168, 180) sts on spare needle that are held parallel to each other

Break yarn, leaving a tail that is approx 4 times the length of neck edge. Thread tail onto a tapestry needle and graft front sts together with back sts.

Left Front Band

Using 4mm circular needle, yarn A, and with RS facing, beg at outer corner of the base of the left neckband and pick up and knit 8 sts along base of neckband, then pick up and knit 1 st near to the inner corner of the base of neckband on left front edge, PM, and pick up and knit 69 (69, 69, 69, 77, 77, 77, 77, 77) sts along the left front edge to bottom edge, making sure to pick up last st as close to the corner as possible. *78 (78, 78, 78, 86, 86, 86, 86, 86) sts*

Row 1 (WS): Sl1 pwise wyif, [p1, k1] to marker, SM, p2tog, turn, leaving rem sts from base of neckband on needle. *1 st dec*
Row 2 (RS): Sl1 kwise wyib, SM, [p1, k1] to last st, k1.
Rep rows 1-2 twice more.
Note: If you do not wish to work buttonholes, skip the next two rows and rep above rows 1-2 once more instead, then continue to *Left Front Band Resumes for all Styles.*

Buttonholes (traditionally done on left side for men's garments)

Buttonhole row (WS): Sl1 pwise wyif, [p1, k1] twice, [cast off 3 sts in patt, work 11 (11, 11, 11, 13, 13, 13, 13, 13) sts in patt counting 1 st on RH needle] 4 times, cast off 3 sts in patt, [p1, k1] twice, SM, p2tog, turn.
Next row (RS): Work as for row 2, using the Backwards-Loop Method to cast on 3 sts over each cast-off buttonhole.

Left Front Band Resumes for all Styles

Rep rows 1-2 a further 3 times. *1 st rem at base of neckband*

Next row (WS): P1, [sl1 pwise wyif, k1] to marker, SM, p2tog. *1 st dec*

Next row (RS): Sl1 pwise wyib, remove marker, [sl1 pwise wyif, k1] to last st, sl1 pwise wyif.

Slipping each st pwise, slip the knit sts onto the working needle and the purl sts onto a spare circular needle, held at the back. The first st on working needle counts as a knit st. *35 (35, 35, 35, 39, 39, 39, 39, 39) sts on each needle*

Break yarn, leaving a tail that is approx 4 times the length of front band edge. Thread tail onto a tapestry needle and with needles held parallel to each other, graft front sts together with back sts.

Right Front Band

Note: Sts are picked up from left to right. If preferred, sts may be picked up and knit from right to left instead, then break yarn and rejoin it at the bottom right corner.

Using 4mm circular needle, yarn A, and with RS facing, beg at outer corner of the base of the right neckband and pick up and knit (working from left to right) 8 sts along base of neckband, then pick up and knit 1 st near to the inner corner of the base of neckband on right front edge, PM, and pick up and knit 69 (69, 69, 69, 77, 77, 77, 77, 77) sts along right front edge to bottom edge, making sure to pick up last st as close to the corner as possible. *78 (78, 78, 78, 86, 86, 86, 86, 86) sts*

Row 1 (RS): Sl1 kwise wyib, [k1, p1] to marker, SM, ssk, turn, leaving rem sts from base of neckband on needle. *1 st dec*
Row 2 (WS): Sl1 pwise wyif, SM, [k1, p1] to last st, p1.
Rep rows 1-2 twice more.
Note: If you do not wish to work buttonholes, skip the next two rows and rep above rows 1-2 once more instead, then continue to *Right Front Band Resumes for all Styles.*

Buttonholes (traditionally done on right side for women's garments)

Buttonhole row (RS): Sl1 kwise wyib, [k1, p1] twice, [cast off 3 sts in patt, work 11 (11, 11, 11, 13, 13, 13, 13, 13) sts in patt counting 1 st on RH needle] 4 times, cast off 3 sts in patt, [k1, p1] twice, SM, ssk, turn.

Next row (WS): Work as for row 2, using the Backwards-Loop Method to cast on 3 sts over each cast off buttonhole.

Right Front Band Resumes for all Styles
Rep rows 1-2 a further 3 times. *1 st rem at base of neckband*
Next row (RS): Sl1 kwise wyib, [k1, sl1 pwise wyif] to marker, SM, ssk. *1 st dec*
Next row (WS): Sl1 pwise wyif, remove marker, [k1, Sl1 pwise wyif,] to last st, k1.

Slipping each st pwise, slip the knit sts onto the working needle and the purl sts onto a spare circular needle, held at the back. The first st on working needle counts as a purl st. *35 (35, 35, 35, 39, 39, 39, 39, 39) sts on each needle*

Break yarn, leaving a tail that is approx 4 times the length of neck edge. Thread tail onto a tapestry needle and with needles held parallel to each other, graft front sts together with back sts.

Pocket Bags (work for each side)
If pocket flap is tucked in, pull it out to the RS of work. Using 5mm needles suitable for working small circumferences, return 26 (26, 26, 26, 28, 28, 28, 28, 28) sts on hold for pocket back onto needle. Join yarn A and k26 (26, 26, 26, 28, 28, 28, 28, 28) sts, pick up and knit 26 (26, 26, 26, 28, 28, 28, 28, 28) sts along pocket flap, PM to indicate beg of round. *52 (52, 52, 52, 56, 56, 56, 56, 56) sts*

Working in St st in the round, work until pocket bag measures 10cm / 4". Push pocket to WS of work. Divide sts onto 2 needles and close with a Three-Needle Cast Off.

Rep for second pocket.

FINISHING
Weave in ends and block flat to measurements. If needed, sew a button to opposite front band to correspond with each buttonhole.

Need help with the pocket construction? Please see the *Ginsan* pocket tutorial at kshandknitdesign.com!

Schematic Measurements
a. Finished chest (fullest point) circumference, including bands: 102 (112, 122, 131, 141, 149, 159, 168, 178)cm / 40 (44, 48, 51½, 55½, 58½, 62½, 66, 70)"

b. Length (hem to underarm): 38 (38, 38, 38, 38, 40.5, 40.5, 40.5, 40.5)cm / 15 (15, 15, 15, 16, 16, 16, 16, 16)"

c. Yoke Depth: 23 (26.5, 28.5, 28.5, 32, 33.5, 35.5, 36, 40)cm / 9 (10.5, 11.25, 11.25, 12.5, 13.25, 14, 14.25, 15.75)"

d. Sleeve length, standard: 33cm / 13"
Sleeve length, tall: 46cm / 18"

e. Upper arm circumference: 34 (38, 43, 44.5, 48, 51, 56, 57, 61)cm / 13½ (15, 17, 17½, 19, 20, 22, 22½, 24)"

f. Back neck width: 16.5 (18, 18, 19, 20.5, 21.5, 21.5, 23, 24)cm / 6½ (7, 7, 7½, 8, 8½, 8½, 9, 9½)"

POKAPOKA

Pokapoka is
a Japanese
onomatopoeia
word used
to describe
feeling warm.

A hat knit in two halves seemed fitting for this book. Each half is essentially worked the same way but in different fibres to create contrasting textures and, in some versions, contrasting colours. It's fully reversible, too. Be sure to check the end of the pattern for a bonus pattern for using your yarn leftovers from this project! ~ *Kiyomi*

If you've ever wondered what the scientific difference is between identical and fraternal twins, it comes down to the egg. A simplistic explanation is that fraternal twins occur when two eggs become fertilised in the same pregnancy, whereas with identical twins, a single fertilised egg miraculously splits and becomes two. Me and Ki are identical twins, each of us half of an egg! This simple hat, knit in two layers, looks like an egg when it's opened up. Each half of the hat is knit with different textured yarn, and it's up to you if you want to choose contrasting colours or keep it in one tone. I personally love the monotone version with the cosy mohair on the inside and then folded up for a fuzzy brim! ~ *Sachiko*

Additional Variation Suggestion
You can knit each half of this hat in the same yarn for a single-coloured hat with no textural change. Try shortening the length even more if you prefer not to have a folded-up brim.

POKAPOKA

Sizes: 1 (2, 3, 4)
Finished circumference: 46.5 (49.5, 52, 55) cm / 18¼ (19½, 20½, 21¾)" - to be worn with approx 6cm / 2½" negative ease

Greg is shown wearing the beanie style with pompom in size 2 on page 38.

Paul is shown wearing the watch cap style with stalk in size 3 on page 37.

Kiyomi is shown wearing the beanie style in size 2 on page 39.

Sachiko is shown wearing the beanie style in size 1 on page 36.

Yarn:
Yarn A: Qing Fibre Merino Single (fingering / 4-ply-weight; 100% superwash merino wool; 366m / 400yds per 100g skein)

Watch Cap: 1 skein, or approx. 150 (165, 175, 190)m / 165 (180, 190, 205)yds of smooth fingering / 4-ply-weight yarn
Beanie: 1 skein, or approx. 200 (215, 230, 250) m / 215 (235, 250, 270) yds of smooth fingering / 4-ply-weight yarn

Yarn B: Qing Fibre Kid Mohair Silk (lace-weight; 70% mohair, 30% silk; 420m / 459yds per 50g skein)

Watch Cap: 1 skein, or approx. 115 (125, 135, 145)m / 125 (135, 145, 160) yds of mohair / fuzzy textured lace-weight yarn
Beanie: 1 skein, or approx. 145 (160, 170, 180)m / 160 (175, 186, 200)yds of mohair / fuzzy textured lace-weight yarn

Shades Shown (Merino Single / Kid Mohair Silk):
Bluefinch Bedrock / Bone - beanie style
Deep Forest / Deep Forest - beanie style
Smoke / Smoke - watch cap with stalk
Hero / Honeycomb - beanie style with pompom

Yarn amounts do not include yarn for pompoms or stalks

Gauge: 28 sts & 40 rows = 10cm / 4" over St st with yarn A (Merino Single) on 3mm needles, after blocking.

28 sts & 36 rows = 10cm / 4" over St st with yarn B (Kid Mohair Silk) on 3mm needles, after blocking.

Be sure to check gauge and block both yarns and adjust needle size as necessary to obtain same stitch gauge for both yarns. You might require a different needle size for each yarn. Please make sure to take note of row gauge, as you will need to know it!

Needles & Hook: 3mm / US 2½ circular needle, 40cm / 16" length AND needles suitable for working small circumferences in the round
3.25mm / US D crochet hook (or larger) for Crochet Provisional Cast-On
Two 3mm / US 2½ double pointed needles for working I-cord stalk (optional)

Always use a needle size that will result in the correct gauge after blocking.

Notions: 4 stitch markers (including one unique for beg of round), smooth waste yarn (for provisional cast-on), tapestry needle, pompom maker (optional)

Notes: The *PokaPoka* Hat is a reversible double layered hat worked in two different textured yarns, and with multiple depths and top finishing choices. It is worked as one piece in the round, but in two sections; like two hats attached together at the bottom. First, one half of the hat is worked from a crocheted provisional cast-on using the Merino Single yarn. Once completed, the provisional cast-on is removed and a second hat is worked in the same manner as the first, but with the Kid Mohair Silk yarn. Once both halves are completed, one hat is tucked inside the other to form a reversible double layered hat. It is important to knit the first half with the smoother yarn (Merino Single) as it is too difficult to see the stitches worked in mohair for removing the provisional cast-on. There are two lengths given for this hat - short for a more fitted watch cap style, and a slouchy beanie style. Choose the length you prefer, noting the difference in yarn requirements. The brim can be folded up to different heights as well, or even double folded or rolled. All will affect the depth of the hat differently. Different top finishings are also given - a basic embellishment-free top, a mini pompom, or a stalk. You can choose different combinations of tops for each half of your hat. Row gauge is essential for making sure both halves of your hat are the same length and will fit neatly inside one another when completed. Different yarn types will yield different row gauges. Please swatch both yarns A and B and be sure to block as yarn can grow. Record the final row gauge for both yarns once the correct stitch gauge is achieved. To calculate the number of rounds needed to work for each half, use the following formula:

Desired hat length before crown shaping (cm or inches) divided by 10cm / 4" multiplied by row gauge from swatch over 10cm / 4" = number of rounds needed

Example (cm): 25cm / 10cm x 40 rows = 100 rounds
Example (inches): 10" / 4" x 40 rows = 100 rounds

PATTERN BEGINS
FIRST HALF (SMOOTH WOOL)
Using crochet hook, circular needle, waste yarn and the Crochet Provisional Cast-On Method, cast on 128 (136, 144, 152) sts. Join yarn A and knit 1 row. Join for working in the round being careful not to twist. PM to indicate beg of round.

Work even in St st in the round until piece measures 20cm / 8" (approx 80 rounds or number of rounds needed for your gauge {see notes}) for watch cap, or 25.5cm / 10" (approx 100 rounds) for beanie from cast-on edge.

SHAPE CROWN
Note: Change to needles suitable for working small circumferences when necessary.
Set-up round: *K32 (34, 36, 38) sts, PM; rep from * 2 more times, k32 (34, 36, 38) sts to end. *3 new markers placed*

Dec round: *K1, k2tog, k to 3 sts before marker, ssk, k1, SM; rep from * 2 more times, k1, k2tog, k to 3 sts before marker, ssk, k1. *8 sts dec*
Next round: Knit, slipping markers as you pass them.
Rep last 2 rounds a further 13 (14, 15, 16) times. *16 sts*

Next round: [K2tog] to end. *8 sts*

For Basic Top ONLY
Break yarn leaving a long tail. Using tapestry needle, thread tail through the rem 8 sts and pull tightly to close.

For Stalk ONLY
Next round: [K2tog] to end. *4 sts*
Place 4 sts onto 1 DPN and knit i-cord for 2.5cm / 1". Break yarn leaving a long tail. Using tapestry needle, thread tail through rem 4 sts and pull tightly to fasten off.

SECOND HALF (MOHAIR)
Carefully undo the provisional cast-on and place sts onto circular needle. With RS facing, join yarn B, and PM to indicate beg of round.
128 (136, 144, 152) on needle

Work even in St st in the round until piece measures 20cm / 8" (approx 72 rounds or number of rounds needed for your gauge {see notes}) for watch cap, or 25.5cm / 10" (approx 90 rounds) for beanie from cast-on edge.

Before commencing crown shaping, weave in ends at yarn change on the WS.

Work crown shaping as for first half.

FINISHING
Do not weave in rem ends. Wet block flat to measurements. When hat is fully dry, fold in half, tucking one half of the hat (either) inside the other, making sure that the bottom fold is aligned with the yarn change.

For the basic top or pompom versions, weave in ends, using ends at the top of crown to attach the two layers together. Make two 2.5cm / 1" pompoms one each in yarns A and B and attach to top centre of crown.

For the stalk, draw tail inside stalk to WS using a tapestry needle. Weave in rem ends.

Fold up brim 5cm / 2" or to preferred height.

Watch Cap: 27 (28, 28.5, 29)cm / 10¾ (11, 11¼, 11½)"

Beanie: 32 (33, 33.5, 34)cm / 12¾ (13, 13¼, 13½)"

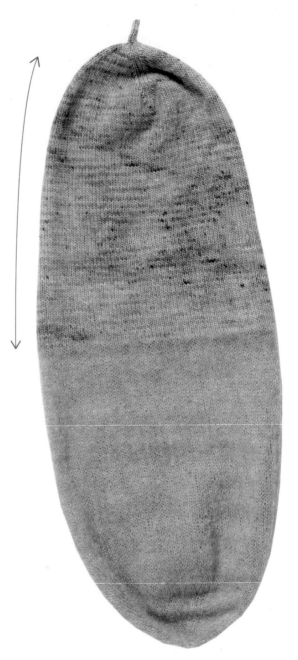

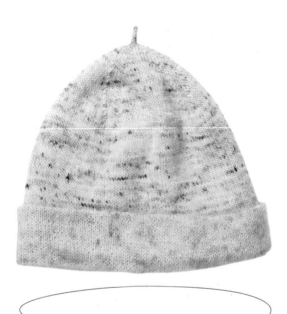

46.5 (49.5, 52, 55)cm / 18¼ (19½, 20½, 21¾)"

Bonus Cowl Pattern!!!

Using the leftover yarn, you can make a simple cowl to match the *PokaPoka* hat! Using the *PokaPoka* hat pattern, cast on sts for desired size.

Work instructions for *First Half* without working Crown Shaping and until piece measures approx 20cm / 8", or until yarn has almost run out. Break yarn, making sure to save at least 5m / 5½yds of yarn A for later and place sts on holders or waste yarn.

Work instructions for *Second Half* without working Crown Shaping until piece measures the same length as first half. Break yarn B, and work 1 more round in St st using the yarn A that was saved. Fold piece in half, bringing the first half inside the second half so that live edges are together with RS facing outwards. Return sts on holders or waste yarn to a spare needle and using yarn A, graft sts together to close.

Weave in ends and block.

TRIONYX

If you are
curious about
the name,
trionyx is
the name
of a breed
of soft-shelled
turtle. These
unique creatures
come in a
multitude
of shell and
skin patterns
and colours.
They are also
known for
their striking
good looks.
One of
these points
is false.

After completing a few knitting projects, you've probably come across the terms gauge or tension, and been instructed numerous times to check it, measure it and adjust needle size, or else face dire consequences. Some of us have learned the hard way. We've been told that a difference in gauge of only half a stitch can make quite a surprising difference to the outcome of the size of a project.

From my own experience, I've found that changing the weight of your yarn from the recommended weight of yarn in a pattern (as long as it's not a really drastic weight difference) actually doesn't alter the gauge as much as you'd expect. If you're using a fingering-weight when a DK-weight is called for in a project, you may actually find that you can achieve quite a close gauge. Of course, the thickness and fibre of your chosen yarn will alter the drape and feel of the finished project.

We've knit the *Trionyx* shawl using a woolly DK-weight and again in a floaty silk mohair, just to see what would happen! It's a fun and interesting experiment to choose yarn with a different fibre or weight to get a completely new effect. A shawl is a great place to conduct this kind of experimentation, where the friendly line "gauge is not essential" may have you skipping to cast on. But on the off chance that you would like to achieve a certain size of shawl, we've made a handy little table for you to use as a guideline. The catch? You have to obtain gauge!
~ *Sachiko*

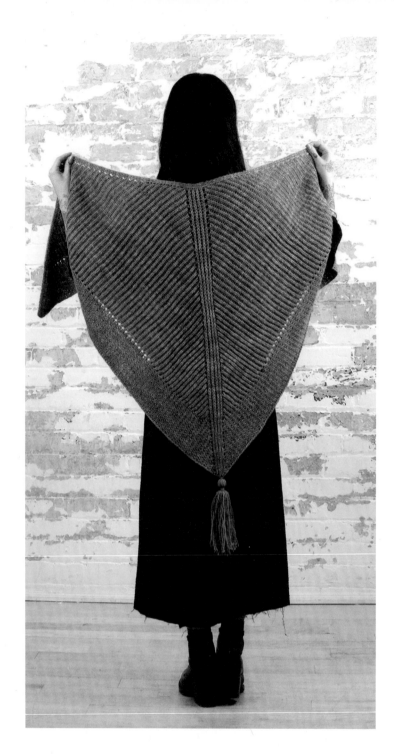

Additional Variation Suggestion
For the DK version, I added a 10cm/ 4″
tassel to the apex of the shawl. Try adding
other embellishments such as fringe along
the edges or pompoms at the corners.

TRIONYX

Size: DK Version: approx 85.5cm / 33¾"
long x 171.5cm / 67½" wide
Mohair Lace Version (Pollen): approx
75cm / 29½" long x 149cm / 58¾" wide
Mohair Lace Version (Midnight): approx
58cm / 22¾ long x 115.5cm / 45½" wide

Kiyomi's height is 155cm / 5'1", and is
shown wearing the Mohair Lace version
in Pollen on pages 44, 45 and 51.

Sachiko's height is 157.5cm / 5'2", and is
shown wearing the DK version on pages 46
and 51.

Greg's height is 173cm / 5'8", and is shown
wearing the Mohair Lace version in
Midnight on page 47.

Size is adjustable (see notes).

Yarn:
DK Version
Viola West Country (DK-weight; 50% Exmoor
Horn wool, 30% Bluefaced Leicester wool,
20% Wensleydale wool; 233m / 255yds per
100g ball/skein)
Shade: Cosmic; 4 skeins for size shown

Mohair Lace Version
Viola Mohair Lace (lace-weight; 72% mohair,
28% silk; 420m / 459yds per 50g skein)
Shade: Pollen; 2 skeins for larger size shown,
Midnight; 1 skein for smaller size shown

Gauge:
DK Version
15 sts & 40 rows = 10cm / 4" over Fisherman's
Rib pattern on 4.5mm needles,
after blocking.

Mohair Lace Version
14 sts & 34 rows = 10cm / 4" over Fisherman's
Rib pattern on 4.5mm needles, after blocking.

Needles: 4.5mm / US 7 circular needle,
100cm / 40" length
5mm / US 8 circular needle, 100cm / 40" length

*Always use a needle size that will result
in the correct gauge after blocking.*

Notions: 4 stitch markers, tapestry needle

Stitch Glossary:
(p1, k1 into yo): With yarn in front, insert
needle from back to front under yo and purl
yo without dropping yo off LH needle. Bring
yarn to back, insert needle from front to back,
knit into yo, and lift yo off of LH needle. *1 st inc*

(k1, p1 into yo): With yarn in back, insert needle
from front to back under yo and knit yo without
dropping yo off of LH needle. Bring yarn to
front, insert needle from the back to front, purl
into yo, and lift yo off of LH needle. *1 st inc*

PATTERN BEGINS
Beginning Tab
With smaller needles, cast on 6 sts.
Row 1 (WS): P2, [k1, p1] twice.
Row 2 (RS): Sl1 pwise wyib, [p1, k1] twice, k1.
Rep rows 1-2 rows a further 3 times.

Without turning work after last row (yarn is
at left hand side), rotate work 90 degrees,
and pick up and knit 7 sts along the side.
Rotate work 90 degrees again, pick up and
knit 6 sts along the cast-on edge. *19 sts*

Set-up row (WS): Sl1 pwise wyif, [k1, p1]
twice, PM, k1, PM, [p1, k1] 3 times, p1, PM,
k1, PM, [p1, k1] twice, p1.
Row 1 (RS): Sl1 kwise wyib, [p1, k1b] twice,
SM, p1, SM, [k1b, p1] 3 times, k1b, SM, p1,
SM, [k1b, p1] twice, k1.
Row 2 (WS)(inc): Sl1 pwise wyif, [k1b, p1] twice,
SM, yo, k1b, yo, SM, [p1, k1b] 3 times, p1, SM,
yo, k1b, yo, SM, [p1, k1b] twice, p1. *23 sts*
Row 3 (RS)(inc): Sl1 kwise wyib, [p1, k1b]
twice, SM, (p1, k1 into yo), p1, (k1, p1 into
yo), SM, [k1b, p1] 3 times, k1b, SM, (p1, k1
into yo), p1, (k1, p1 into yo), SM, [k1b, p1]
twice, k1. *27 sts*
Row 4 (WS): Sl1 pwise wyif, [k1b, p1] twice,
SM, k1, p1, k1b, p1, k1, SM, [p1, k1b] 3 times,
p1, SM, k1, p1, k1b, p1, k1, SM, [p1, k1b]
twice, p1.
Row 5 (RS): Sl1 kwise wyib, [p1, k1b] twice,
SM, [p1, k1b] to last st before marker, p1, SM,
[k1b, p1] 3 times, k1b, SM, [p1, k1b] to last st
before marker, p1, SM, [p1, k1b] twice, k1.

Row 6 (WS)(inc): Sl1 pwise wyif, [k1b, p1] twice, SM, yo, [k1b, p1] to last st before marker, k1b, yo, SM, [p1, k1b] 3 times, p1, SM, yo, [k1b, p1] to last st before marker, k1b, yo, SM, [p1, k1b] twice, p1. *4 sts inc*

Row 7 (RS)(inc): Sl1 kwise wyib, [p1, k1b] twice, SM, (p1, k1 into yo), [p1, k1b] to last st before yo, p1, (k1, p1 into yo), SM [k1b, p1] 3 times, k1b, SM, (p1, k1 into yo), [p1, k1b] to last st before yo, p1, (k1, p1 into yo), SM, [k1b, p1] twice, k1. *4 sts inc*

Row 8 (WS): Sl 1 pwise wyif, [k1b, p1] twice, SM, k1, p1, [k1b, p1] to 3 sts before marker, k1b, p1, k1, SM, [p1, k1b] 3 times, p1, SM, k1, p1, [k1b, p1] to 3 sts before marker, k1b, p1, k1, SM, [p1, k1b] twice, p1.

For DK Version:
Rep rows 5-8 a further 37 times OR see table on page 50 for repeat adjustments**. Work row 5 only once more. *331 sts; 39 yos down each side of center spine*

For Mohair Lace Version:
Rep rows 5-8 a further 28 times (for Shawl shown in Pollen) OR 19 times (for Shawl shown in Midnight) OR see table on page 50 for repeat adjustments**.
Work row 5 only once more. *259 (187) sts; 30 (21) yos down each side of center spine*

Edging
Change to larger needle.
Set-up row 1 (WS): Sl1 pwise wyif, [k1, p1] twice, SM, [yo, ssp] to last st before marker, k1, yo, SM, [p1, k1] 3 times, p1, SM, yo, k1, [p2tog, yo] to marker, SM, [p1, k1] twice, p1. *2 sts inc*
Set-up row 2 (RS): Sl1 kwise wyib, [p1, k1] twice, SM, (k1, p1 into yo), [k1, p1] to last st before marker, (k1, p1 into yo), SM, [k1, p1] 3 times, k1, SM, (p1, k1 into yo), [p1, k1] to last st before marker, (p1, k1 into yo), SM, [k1, p1] twice, k1. *4 sts inc*

Row 1 (WS): Sl1 pwise wyif, [k1, p1] twice, SM, p to marker, SM, [p1, k1] 3 times, p1, SM, p to marker, SM, [p1, k1] twice, p1.
Row 2 (RS): Sl1 kwise wyib, [p1, k1] twice, SM, [k1, p1] to marker, SM, [k1, p1] 3 times, k1, SM, [p1, k1] to marker, SM, [k1, p1] twice, k1.

Row 3 (WS)(inc): Sl1 pwise wyif, [k1, p1] twice, SM, yo, p to marker, yo, SM, [p1, k1] 3 times, p1, SM, yo, p to marker, yo, SM, [p1, k1] twice, p1. *4 sts inc*
Row 4 (RS)(inc): Sl1 kwise wyib, [p1, k1] twice, SM, (k1, p1 into yo), [k1, p1] to last st before marker, (k1, p1 into yo), SM, [k1, p1] 3 times, k1, SM, (p1, k1 into yo), [p1, k1] to last st before marker, (p1, k1 into yo), SM, [k1, p1] twice, k1. *4 sts inc*
Rep rows 1-4 a further 6 times, then work row 1 only once more. *393 sts for DK Version, 321 (249) sts for Mohair Lace Version*

Cast off loosely.

FINISHING
Weave in ends and block.

Tassel (optional)
With scrap cardboard, cut out a rectangle approx 20.5cm / 8" long and 7.5cm / 3" wide. Wrap yarn lengthwise around the cardboard until half of the desired tassel thickness is reached on one side of the cardboard. Make sure not to wrap too tightly. Break yarn. Thread tapestry needle with a length of yarn 25.5cm / 10" long and use it to tightly tie around yarn strands together, close to the top of cardboard. At the opposite end of cardboard, cut yarn strands and remove from cardboard. Approx 2.5cm / 1" down from the top tie, take a 46cm / 18" length of yarn and wrap it tightly around yarn strands 5-10 times. Tie knot and bury ends inside tassel. Trim ends of tassel and attach to shawl's apex.

To adjust the size of the shawl, when you reach ** in the pattern, please repeat rows 5-8, the instructed number of times more below. It is important to follow these numbers of repeats in order to have the correct number of stitches for working the edging. Please ensure you have obtained the gauge specified in pattern.

For a DK Shawl with an approx Wingspan of:	Rep Rows 5-8, this many MORE times	Stitch count before Edging	Final stitch count before bind off	Skeins of Viola Yarns West Country	Approx meterage / yardage needed
87cm / 34¼"	13	139	201	1	220m / 240yds
98cm / 38½"	16	163	225	2	270m / 300yds
109cm / 42¾"	19	187	249	2	340m / 370yds
119cm / 46¾"	22	211	273	2	400m / 445yds
129cm / 50¾"	25	235	297	3	475m / 520yds
140.5cm / 55¼"	28	259	321	3	555m / 610yds
150.5cm / 59¼"	31	283	345	3	645m / 710yds
161.5cm / 63½"	34	307	369	4	730m / 805yds
171.5cm / 67½"*	37	331	393	4	830m / 915yds
181.5cm / 71½"	40	355	417	4	925m / 1015yds
192.5cm / 75¾"	43	379	441	5	1045m / 1150yds
203cm / 80"	46	403	465	6	1170m / 1285yds

For a MOHAIR Shawl with an approx Wingspan of:	Rep Rows 5-8, this many MORE times	Stitch count before Edging	Final stitch count before bind off	Skeins of Viola Yarns Mohair Lace	Approx meterage/ yardage needed
93.5cm / 36¾"	13	139	201	1	180m / 200yds
104cm / 41"	16	163	225	1	225m / 245yds
115.5cm / 45½ "*	19	187	249	1	275m / 300yds
126.5cm / 49¾"	22	211	273	1	325m / 360yds
138cm / 54¼"	25	235	297	1	390m / 425yds
149.5cm / 58¾"*	28	259	321	2	455m / 500yds
160cm / 63"	31	283	345	2	520m / 570yds
172cm / 67¾"	34	307	369	2	600m / 660yds
184cm / 72½"	37	331	393	2	690m / 755yds
194.5cm / 76½"	40	355	417	2	760m / 835yds
206cm / 81"	43	379	441	3	855m / 940yds
217cm / 85½ "	46	403	465	3	950m / 1045yds

*This size is shown in photos.

ZENER

You may recognise the colourwork motif on these socks from two other designs in this collection, the *ESP* toque and the *Kordy* yoke sweater. When I saw it on the *ESP* toque, I knew I wanted to try it on a sock, so I borrowed it from Ki's design. What better opportunity would I have to take a design from my sis and get away with it?

In the last few years, I've really started to enjoy knitting socks. When I was a new knitter, I found the small needles and thin yarn a daunting prospect, but quickly found that the slim materials were really the least of my concerns. Enter second sock syndrome. I've heard various strategies and techniques on how to beat this crafting ailment, such as two at a time etc. My fave tip? It's a simple concept, really. It works great for anyone who uses DPNs and has worked for me so far! Here goes. As soon as you're done the first sock, cast on the second sock immediately and work at least 1-2 rounds. Do it right away! That's it. And hopefully having it ready to go on the needles will be enough of an encouragement to keep you knitting. Alternatively, you could just keep knitting singleton socks and have a drawer full of mismatches...up to you! ~ *Sachiko*

Chi took my design idea but I don't mind because I really dislike knitting socks. ~ *Kiyomi*

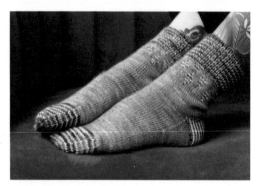

As a companion design to the *ESP* toque, we named these socks *Zener*, which comes from the Zener cards that were used in the 1930s to conduct experiments for extrasensory perception.

ZENER

Sizes: 1 (2, 3)
Finished leg and foot circumference: 19 (23, 27)cm / 7½ (9, 10½)"
Leg length: 12.5cm / 5"

Sachiko and Kiyomi's foot circumference is 20.5cm / 8", and are both shown wearing size 2 on pages 52, 53 and 57.

Paul's foot circumference is 23cm / 9", and is shown wearing size 3 on page 57.

Yarn: Akara Yarn Merino Sock (fingering / 4-ply-weight; 80% merino, 20% nylon; 384m / 420yds per 115g skein)

Yarn A: 1 skein OR approx. 220 (236, 275)m / 240 (260, 300)yds of fingering / 4-ply-weight yarn
Yarn B: 1 skein OR approx. 35 (50, 70)m / 40 (55, 75)yds of fingering / 4-ply-weight yarn
Yarn C: 1 skein OR approx. 35 (50, 70)m / 40 (55, 75)yds of fingering / 4-ply-weight yarn

Shades Shown:
Sample 1, shown in size 2
Yarn A: Rose Gold
Yarn B: Incense
Yarn C: Toasted Marshmallow

Sample 2, shown in size 3
Yarn A: Willow
Yarn B: Honey Bear
Yarn C: Nougat

Sample 3, shown in size 2
Yarn A: Rusty Bucket
Yarn B: Plum
Yarn C: Rose Gold

Gauge: 32 sts & 46 rows = 10cm / 4" over St st on larger needles, after blocking.

Needles: 2mm / US 0 needles suitable for working small circumferences in the round
2.25mm / US 1 needles suitable for working small circumferences in the round

Always use a needle size that will result in the correct gauge after blocking.

Notions: Stitch marker, tapestry needle

PATTERN BEGINS
Using smaller needles, yarn B, and your preferred stretchy cast-on method, cast on 60 (72, 84) sts. Join in the round, being careful not to twist sts. PM to indicate beg of round.

Join yarn C. Do not break yarns between colour changes.
Round 1: With yarn C, work in 1x1 Rib.
Rounds 2-3: With yarn B, work in 1x1 Rib.
Rep rounds 1-3 a further 6 times. Do not break yarns.

LEG
Change to larger needles.
Next round: Working from the Chart for your size, work round 1 of Chart 6 times to end. Continue working from Chart as set through round 18. Break yarns B and C.

Using yarn A only, knit until leg measures approx 12.5cm / 5" from cast-on edge.

HEEL FLAP
Left Sock ONLY
Break yarn A and join yarn B. Turn work so that WS is facing you. Heel flap is worked back and forth in rows.
Set-up row (WS): P2 with yarn B, [p1 with yarn C, p1 with yarn B] 12 (15, 18) times, until 26 (32, 38) sts have been worked, p1 with yarn C, p2 with yarn B. *29 (35, 41) heel flap sts*

Right Sock ONLY
Next round: With yarn A, k29 (35, 41) sts, leaving the rem sts unworked. Turn work so that WS is facing you, break yarn A and join yarn B. Heel flap is worked back and forth in rows.
Set-up row (WS): [K1, p1] with yarn B, [p1 with yarn C, p1 with yarn B] 12 (15, 18) times, until 26 (32, 38) sts have been worked, p1 with yarn C, [p1, k1] with yarn B. *29 (35, 41) heel flap sts*

BOTH Socks Continue
Without breaking yarns, continue to work back and forth in rows on these 29 (35, 41) sts only to form the heel flap as follows:

Row 1 (RS): K2 with yarn B, [k1 with yarn C, k1 with yarn B] to last 3 sts of heel flap, k1 with yarn C, k2 with yarn B. *29 (35, 41) heel flap sts*
Row 2 (WS): [K1, p1] with yarn B, [p1 with yarn C, p1 with yarn B] to last 3 sts of heel flap, p1 with yarn C, [p1, k1] with yarn B.
Rep rows 1-2 a further 8 (9, 10) times. Break yarn C. *19 (21, 23) rows worked for heel flap*

TURN HEEL
Note: All sl sts should be slipped pwise from this point on, with yarn held in front on WS rows, and yarn held at back for RS rows.

With yarn B, working over 29 (35, 41) heel flap sts, continue as foll:
Row 1 (RS): Sl1, k15 (19, 23), ssk, k1, turn.
Row 2 (WS): Sl1, p4 (6, 8), p2tog, p1, turn.
Row 3 (RS): Sl1, k5 (7, 9), ssk, k1, turn.
Row 4 (WS): Sl1, p6 (8, 10), p2tog, p1, turn.
Row 5 (RS): Sl1, k7 (9, 11), ssk, k1, turn.
Row 6 (WS): Sl1, p8 (10, 12), p2tog, p1, turn.
Row 7 (RS): Sl1, k9 (11, 13), ssk, k1, turn.
Row 8 (WS): Sl1, p10 (12, 14), p2tog, p1, turn.
Row 9 (RS): Sl1, k11 (13, 15), ssk, k1, turn.
Row 10 (WS): Sl1, p12 (14, 16), p2tog, p1, turn.
Row 11 (RS): Sl1, k13 (15, 17), ssk, k1, turn.
Row 12 (WS): Sl1, p14 (16, 18), p2tog, p1, turn. *17 (23, 29) sts*

Size 2 ONLY:
Row 13 (RS): Sl1, k17, ssk, k1, turn.
Row 14 (WS): Sl1, p18, p2tog, p1, turn. *21 sts*

Size 3 ONLY:
Row 13 (RS): Sl1, k19, ssk, turn.
Row 14 (WS): Sl1, p20, p2tog, turn.
Row 15 (RS): Sl1, k21, ssk, turn.
Row 16 (WS): Sl1, p22, p2tog, p1, turn. *25 sts*

ALL sizes again:
Break yarn B and join yarn A.
Set-up round (RS): Using yarn A, k8 (10, 12) heel sts, PM for new beg of round, k9 (11, 13) rem heel sts, pick up and knit 14 (16, 18) sts up side of heel flap, PM, k31 (37, 43) instep sts, PM, pick up and knit 14 (16, 18) sts down side of heel flap, knit to end of round. *76 (90, 104) sts*
Knit 1 round.

GUSSET SHAPING
Round 1 (dec): Knit to 3 sts before marker, k2tog, k1, SM, knit across instep sts to next marker, SM, k1, ssk, knit to end. *2 sts dec*
Round 2: Knit.
Rep rounds 1-2 a further 7 (8, 9) times. *60 (72, 84) sts*

Work even in St st until foot measures approx 4 (5, 5.5)cm / 1½ (2, 2¼)" less than desired foot length.

Next round: Remove beg of round marker, knit to next marker. This marker will be the new beg of round. Break yarn A and join yarn B.
Next round: Using yarn B, k30 (36, 42), PM for side, k1, remove previous side marker, knit to end.

TOE SHAPING
Round 1 (dec): Using yarn B, *k1, ssk, knit to 3 sts before marker, k2tog, k1; rep from * once more. *4 sts dec*
Round 2: Using yarn C, knit to end.
Work Dec round every other round, and AT THE SAME TIME alternate between 2 rounds of yarn B and 1 round of yarn C. Once 8 (11, 12) dec rounds have been worked and 28 (28, 36) sts rem, break yarn C and continue with yarn B only. Work Dec round every other round a further 1 (1, 2) times. *24 (24, 28) sts*

Knit 1 round even. Rearrange stitches so there are 12 (12, 14) sts on each of 2 needles at top and bottom of foot.
Cut yarn leaving a long tail, and graft top and bottom stitches together.

FINISHING
Weave in ends and block to measurements.

Z
E
N
E
R

Chart - Size 1 ONLY

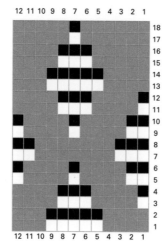

Chart - Size 2 ONLY

Chart - Size 3 ONLY

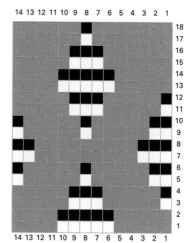

Key

■ Knit with yarn A

■ Knit with yarn B

☐ Knit with yarn C

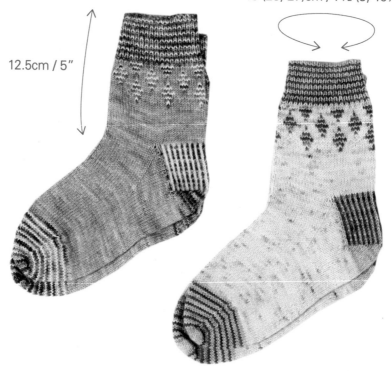

12.5cm / 5"

19 (23, 27)cm / 7½ (9, 10½)"

CESIUM REDUX

Jules Piccard
was a chemist
and student
of the scientists
who discovered
the element
cesium (Robert
Bunsen and
Gustav Kirchhoff).
His twin sons
were Auguste
and Jean-Felix
Piccard, who
became scientists
as well as
famous
high-altitude
balloonists
who studied
the Earth's
atmosphere.
The original
Cesium was
named back
in 2016 but
we were able
to connect it
to our book
theme with a
little research.
We felt we
had to mention
these twins
because our
favourite
Star Trek
captain was
named after
the both
of them!

When I made the first *Cesium* sweater for Issue 19 of *Pom Pom Quarterly*, I wanted to create a pullover with a cable that was slightly obscure and asymmetrical. There is generally a lot of symmetry in knitting and many (but not all) classic cabled sweaters are very symmetrical, which serves functionality as well as aesthetic. For *Cesium*, however, my intention was to have a cable pattern that was subtle and looked slightly off-kilter.

Some knitters may not realise that the design timeline from proposal to finished sample for most publications doesn't leave much room for tweaking, especially considering how long knitting actually takes. So admittedly, there have been a few times where a finished, published design of mine stares back at me from the printed page with some glaring design flaws. *Cesium* is thankfully not an example of this but there were some changes I wanted to try and it's not often that a designer gets a second go at a pattern. I've made a few updates, including a broader size range, ribbed hems and a crew neck. There are also now instructions to make it cardiganised! ~ *Sachiko*

I knit the original version of *Cesium* as my wedding sweater. Yes, I got married in a white wool sweater instead of a dress. Do I regret it? Sometimes! But I don't regret knitting *Cesium* because, even after my wedding day, it has become a favourite sweater that gets worn often and evokes fun, warm (and fuzzy) memories. ~ *Kiyomi*

Additional Variation Suggestion
Changing the body length of a sweater
can really affect its overall look. Imagine
making the pullover cropped, or knitting
the cardigan longer to be more like a
light coat! Yarn amounts will need to
be adjusted accordingly.

CESIUM REDUX

Sizes: 1 (2, 3, 4, 5, 6, 7, 8, 9)
Finished chest circumference: 84 (95.5, 104, 115.5, 124.5, 136, 145, 156.5, 165)cm / 33 (37½, 41, 45½, 49, 53½, 57, 61½, 65)" – to be worn with 7.5-12.5cm / 3-5" positive ease.

Paul's height is 175cm / 5'9", with a chest circumference of 91.5cm / 36", and is shown wearing size 4 on pages 60, 62 and 63, with length for taller individuals and longer collar.

Kiyomi's height is 155cm / 5'1", with a chest circumference of 84cm / 33", and is shown wearing size 2 on pages 61 and 69, with standard length.

Sachiko's height is 157.5cm / 5'2", with a chest circumference of 76cm / 30", and is shown wearing size 2 on pages 58, 59, 61 and 63, with standard length.

Yarn: Green Mountain Spinnery Mountain Mohair (worsted-weight; 40% Targhee wool, 30% Mohair, 30% wool; 128m / 140yds per 57g skein)

Pullover: 7 (8, 8, 9, 10, 11, 13, 14, 15) skeins
Shown in shade: Maritime (6815)
Tall Pullover: 7 (8, 9, 10, 11, 12, 14, 15, 16) skeins

Cardigan: 7 (8, 9, 10, 11, 13, 14, 15, 16) skeins
Shown in shade: Spice (6851)
Tall Cardigan: 8 (9, 10, 11, 12, 13, 14, 16, 17) skeins
Shown in shade: Alpenglo (9427)

OR
Pullover: 800 (911, 1023, 1154, 1267, 1400, 1559, 1689, 1820)m / 875 (997, 1119, 1262, 1386, 1532, 1705, 1848, 1991)yds of worsted-weight yarn

For Tall pullover, an additional: 69 (79, 87, 96, 106, 116, 136, 144)m / 76 (86, 95, 105, 116, 127, 138, 149, 157)yds of worsted-weight yarn

Cardigan: 889 (1017, 1129, 1278, 1394, 1547, 1706, 1857, 1986)m / 973 (1113, 1235, 1398, 1525, 1692, 1866, 2032, 2173)yds of worsted-weight yarn

For Tall cardigan, an additional: 52 (59, 64, 70, 76, 82, 88, 94, 100)m / 57 (64, 70, 77, 83, 90, 96, 103, 109)yds of worsted-weight yarn

Gauge: 18 sts & 24 rows = 10 cm / 4" over stocking stitch with larger needle after blocking. One 27-st rep of Cable A = 11.5cm / 4½" wide

Needles: 4.5mm / US 7 circular needle, 80-100cm / 32-40" length (depending on size worked) AND 40 cm / 16" length for pullover only
5mm / US 8 circular needle, 80-100cm / 32-40" length (depending on size worked)

Always use a needle size that will result in the correct gauge after blocking.

Notions: 2 stitch markers, cable needle, tapestry needle, **Cardigan only:** 1.5cm / ½" buttons, 8 for standard length version, 9 for Tall version

Notes: Cesium Redux is a cabled pullover or cardigan worked flat in pieces from the bottom up and seamed.

Stitch Glossary:
Cable Pattern A (worked over 27 sts)
Row 1 (RS): K3, 3/3 LC, k3, 3/3 LC, 3/3 RC, k3.
Row 2 (WS): Purl.
Rows 3-6: Work in St st.
Row 7: 3/3 RC, k3, 3/3 RC, k6, 3/3 LC.
Rows 8-12: Work in St st.
Row 13: 3/3 RC, k3, 3/3 RC, k6, 3/3 LC.
Rows 14-18: Work in St st.
Rep rows 1-18 for patt.

Cable Pattern B (worked over 18 sts)
Row 1 (RS): Knit.
Row 2 (WS): Purl.
Rows 3-4: Work in St st.
Row 5: K3, 3/3 LC, 3/3 RC, k3.
Rows 6-10: Work in St st.
Row 11: 3/3 RC, k6, 3/3 LC.
Rows 12-16: Work in St st.
Row 17: 3/3 RC, k6, 3/3 LC.
Row 18: Purl.
Rep rows 1-18 for patt.

Cable Pattern C (worked over 9 sts)
Row 1 (RS): K3, 3/3 LC.
Row 2 (WS): Purl.

Rows 3-6: Work in St st.
Row 7: 3/3 RC, k3.
Rows 8-12: Work in St st.
Row 13: 3/3 RC, k3.
Rows 14-18: Work in St st.
Rep rows 1-18 for patt.

Cable Pattern D (worked over 18 sts)
Row 1 (RS): K3, 3/3 LC, 3/3 RC, k3.
Row 2 (WS): Purl.
Rows 3-6: Work in St st.
Row 7: 3/3 RC, k6, 3/3 LC.
Rows 8-12: Work in St st.
Row 13: 3/3 RC, k6, 3/3 LC.
Rows 14-18: Work in St st.
Rep rows 1-18 for patt.

PATTERN BEGINS
PULLOVER AND CARDIGAN

BACK
** Using smaller needles and Long-Tail
Method, cast on 82 (92, 100, 110, 118, 128,
136, 146, 154) sts.
Row 1 (WS): P1, [k1, p1] to last st, p1.
Row 2 (RS): K2, [p1, k1] to end.
Rep rows 1-2 until piece measures 5cm / 2"
from cast-on edge, ending with a WS row.

Change to larger needles.
Next row (RS)(inc): Kfb, k26 (31, 35, 40, 44,
49, 53, 58, 62), PM, k27, PM, knit to end. *83
(93, 101, 111, 119, 129, 137, 147, 155) sts*
Next row (WS): Purl.
Next row (RS): Knit to marker, SM, work row 1
of Cable patt A over next 27 sts, SM, knit to end.
Next row (WS): Purl to marker, SM, work
next row of Cable patt A over next 27 sts,
SM, purl to end.

Work in patt as set, working next row of
Cable patt A between markers each time,
until piece measures 38 (39.5, 40.5, 42, 43,
44.5, 45, 47, 48.5)cm / 15 (15½, 16, 16½, 17,
17½, 18, 18½, 19)" for standard length or 43
(44.5, 45, 47, 48.5, 49.5, 51, 52, 53.5)cm / 17
(17½, 18, 18½, 19, 19½, 20, 20½, 21)" for tall
length, from cast-on edge, ending with a
WS row.

Shape Armholes
Continuing to work Cable patt A between
markers, cast off 5 (6, 6, 8, 8, 9, 9, 10, 10)
sts at beg of next 2 rows. *73 (81, 89, 95,
103, 111, 119, 127, 135) sts*

Dec row (RS): K2, k2tog, work in patt
to last 4 sts, ssk, k2. *2 sts dec*
Rep Dec row every RS row a further 4
(5, 7, 8, 9, 11, 14, 15, 16) times. *63 (69,
73, 77, 83, 87, 89, 95, 101) sts* **
Work even in patt until piece measures
18 (19, 20.5, 23, 24, 25.5, 27, 28, 29.5)cm
/ 7 (7½, 8, 9, 9½, 10, 10½, 11, 11½)" from
armhole cast-off, ending with a WS row.

Shape Back Neck
Cast off 7 (8, 9, 10, 11, 12, 13, 14, 15) sts at
beg of next 2 rows. *49 (53, 55, 57, 61, 63,
63, 67, 71) sts*
Cast off 7 (9, 10, 10, 12, 13, 13, 14, 16) sts
at beg of following 2 rows. *35 (35, 35,
37, 37, 37, 37, 39, 39) sts*
Cast off rem sts.

Pullover ONLY:
FRONT
Work as for Back from ** to **.
Work even in patt until piece measures
10 (11.5, 12.5, 15, 16.5, 18, 19, 20.5, 21.5)
cm / 4 (4½, 5, 6, 6½, 7, 7½, 8, 8½)" from
armhole cast-off, ending with a WS row.

Shape Front Neck
Next row (RS): K24 (27, 29, 30, 33, 35, 36,
38, 41) sts, cast off centre 15 (15, 15, 17,
17, 17, 17, 19, 19) sts, removing markers
as you encounter them, knit to end.
Work each side of neck separately.

Shape Right Neck
Next row (WS): Purl to last 2 sts, p2tog. *1 st dec*
Next row (RS): Sl1 kwise, cast off 2 sts,
knit to end. *2 sts dec*
Rep last 2 rows once more. *18 (21, 23, 24,
27, 29, 30, 32, 35) sts*

Next row (WS): Purl to last 2 sts, p2tog. *1 st dec*
Next row (RS): Sl1 kwise, k1, pass sl st over,
knit to end. *1 st dec*
Rep last 2 rows once more. *14 (17, 19, 20, 23,
25, 26, 28, 31) sts*

Work even until piece measures 18 (19, 20.5, 23, 24, 25.5, 27, 28, 29.5)cm / 7 (7½, 8, 9, 9½, 10, 10½, 11, 11½)" from armhole cast-off, ending with a RS row.

Shape Right Shoulder
Next row (WS): Cast off 7 (8, 9, 10, 11, 12, 13, 14, 15) sts, p to end. *7 (9, 10, 10, 12, 13, 13, 14, 16) sts*
Next row (RS): Knit.
Cast off rem sts.

Shape Left Neck
With WS facing, join yarn at neck edge.
Next row (WS): Sl1 pwise, cast off 2 sts, purl to end. *2 sts dec*
Next row (RS): Knit to last 2 sts, ssk. *1 st dec*
Rep last 2 rows once more. *18 (21, 23, 24, 27, 29, 30, 32, 35) sts*

Next row (WS): Sl1 pwise, p1, pass sl st over, purl to end. *1 st dec*
Next row (RS): Knit to last 2 sts, ssk. *1 st dec*
Rep last 2 rows once more. *14 (17, 19, 20, 23, 25, 26, 28, 31) sts*

Work even until piece measures 18 (19, 20.5, 23, 24, 25.5, 27, 28, 29.5)cm / 7 (7½, 8, 9, 9½, 10, 10½, 11,11½)" from armhole cast-off, ending with a WS row.

Shape Left Shoulder
Next row (RS): Cast off 7 (8, 9, 10, 11, 12, 13, 14, 15) sts, knit to end. *7 (9, 10, 10, 12, 13, 13, 14, 16) sts*
Next row (WS): Purl.
Cast off rem sts.

Cardigan ONLY:
LEFT FRONT
Using smaller needles and Long-Tail Method, cast on 42 (46, 50, 56, 60, 64, 68, 74, 78) sts.
Row 1 (WS): P1, [k1, p1] to last st, p1.
Row 2 (RS): K2, [p1, k1] to end.
Rep rows 1-2 until piece measures 5cm / 2" from cast-on edge, ending with a WS row.

Change to larger needles.
Next row (RS): Kfb 0 (1, 1, 0, 0, 1, 1, 0, 0) time, knit to last 10 sts, PM, k9, PM, k1. *42 (47, 51, 56, 60, 65, 69, 74, 78) sts*
Next row (WS): Purl.
Next row (RS): Knit to marker, SM, work row 1 of Cable patt C over next 9 sts, SM, k1.

Next row (WS): P1, SM, work next row of Cable patt C over next 9 sts, SM, purl to end.

Work straight in patt as set, working next row of Cable patt C between markers each time, until piece measures 38 (39.5, 40.5, 42, 43 44.5, 45, 47, 48.5)cm / 15 (15½, 16, 16½, 17, 17½, 18, 18½, 19)" for standard length or 43 (44.5, 45, 47, 48.5, 49.5, 51, 52, 53.5)cm / 17 (17½, 18, 18½,19, 19½, 20, 20½, 21)" for tall length, from cast-on edge, ending with a WS row.

Shape Armholes
Next row (RS): Cast off 5 (6, 6, 8, 8, 9, 9, 10, 10) sts, patt to end. *37 (41, 45, 48, 52, 56, 60, 64, 68) sts*
Next row (WS): Patt to end.

Dec row (RS): K2, k2tog, patt to end. *1 st dec*
Next row (WS): Patt to end.
Rep Dec row every RS row a further 4 (5, 7, 8, 9, 11, 14, 15, 16) times. *32 (35, 37, 39, 42, 44, 45, 48, 51) sts*

Work even in patt until piece measures 10 (11.5, 12.5, 15, 16.5, 18, 19, 20.5, 21.5)cm / 4 (4½, 5, 6, 6½, 7, 7½, 8, 8½)" from armhole cast-off, ending with a RS row.

Shape Left Front Neck
Next row (WS): Cast off 8 (8, 8, 9, 9, 9, 9, 10, 10) sts, removing markers as you encounter them, purl to end. *24 (27, 29, 30, 33, 35, 36, 38, 41) sts*
Next row (RS): Knit to last 2 sts, ssk. *1 st dec*
Next row (WS): Sl1 pwise, cast off 2 sts, purl to end. *2 sts dec*
Rep last 2 rows once more. *18 (21, 23, 24, 27, 29, 30, 32, 35) sts*

Next row (RS): Knit to last 2 sts, ssk. *1 st dec*
Next row (WS): Sl1 pwise, p1, pass sl st over, purl to end. *1 st dec*
Rep last 2 rows once more. *14 (17, 19, 20, 23, 25, 26, 28, 31) sts*

Work even until piece measures 18 (19, 20.5, 23, 24, 25.5, 27, 28, 29.5)cm / 7 (7½, 8, 9, 9½, 10, 10½, 11, 11½)" from armhole cast-off, ending with a WS row.

Shape Left Shoulder
Next row (RS): Cast off 7 (8, 9, 10, 11, 12, 13, 14, 15) sts, k to end. *7 (9, 10, 10, 12, 13, 13, 14, 16) sts*
Next row (WS): Purl.
Cast off rem sts.

RIGHT FRONT
Using smaller needles and Long-Tail Method, cast on 42 (46, 50, 56, 60, 64, 68, 74, 78) sts.
Row 1 (WS): P1, [k1, p1] to last st, p1.
Row 2 (RS): K2, [p1, k1] to end.
Rep rows 1-2 until piece measures 5cm / 2" from cast-on edge, ending with a WS row.

Change to larger needles.
Next row (RS): K1, PM, k18, PM, knit to last 0 (1, 1, 0, 0, 1, 1, 0, 0) st, kfb 0 (1, 1, 0, 0, 1, 1, 0, 0) time. *42 (47, 51, 56, 60, 65, 69, 74, 78) sts*
Next row (WS): Purl.
Next row (RS): K1, SM, work row 1 of Cable patt D over next 18 sts, SM, knit to end.
Next row (WS): Purl to marker, SM, work next row of Cable patt D over next 18 sts, SM, p1.

Work in patt as set, working next row of Cable patt D between markers each time, until piece measures 38 (39.5, 40.5, 42, 43, 44.5, 45, 47, 48.5)cm / 15 (15½, 16, 16½, 17, 17½, 18, 18½, 19)" for standard length or 43 (44.5, 45, 47, 48.5, 49.5, 51, 52, 53.5)cm / 17 (17½, 18, 18½, 19, 19½, 20, 20½, 21)" for tall length, from cast-on edge, ending with a RS row.

Shape Armholes
Next row (WS): Cast off 5 (6, 6, 8, 8, 9, 9, 10, 10) sts, patt to end. *37 (41, 45, 48, 52, 56, 60, 64, 68) sts*

Dec row (RS): K1, SM, work next row of cable patt, SM, k to last 4 sts, ssk, k2. *1 st dec*
Next row (WS): Patt to end.
Rep Dec row every RS row a further 4 (5, 7, 8, 9, 11, 14, 15, 16) times. *32 (35, 37, 39, 42, 44, 45, 48, 51) sts*

Work even in patt until piece measures 10 (11.5, 12.5, 15, 16.5, 18, 19, 20.5, 21.5) cm / 4 (4½, 5, 6, 6½, 7, 7½, 8, 8½)" from armhole cast-off, ending with a WS row.

Shape Right Front Neck
Next Row (RS): Cast off 8 (8, 8, 9, 9, 9, 9, 10, 10) sts, removing markers as you encounter them, knit to end. *24 (27, 29, 30, 33, 35, 36, 38, 41) sts*
Next row (WS): Purl to last 2 sts, p2tog. *1 st dec*
Next row (RS): Sl1 pwise, cast off 2 sts, knit to end. *2 sts dec*
Next row (WS): Purl to last 2 sts, p2tog. *1 st dec*
Rep last 2 rows once more. *17 (20, 22, 23, 26, 28, 29, 31, 34) sts*

Next row (RS): Sl1 pwise, k1, pass sl st over next st, knit to end. *1 st dec*
Next row (WS): Purl to last 2 sts, p2tog. *1 st dec*
Next row (RS): Sl1 pwise, k1, pass sl st over next st, knit to end. *14 (17, 19, 20, 23, 25, 26, 28, 31) sts*

Work even until piece measures 18 (19, 20.5, 23, 24, 25.5, 27, 28, 29.5)cm / 7 (7½, 8, 9, 9½, 10, 10½, 11, 11½)" from armhole cast-off, ending with a RS row.

Shape Right Shoulder
Next row (WS): Cast off 7 (8, 9, 10, 11, 12, 13, 14, 15) sts, purl to end. *7 (9, 10, 10, 12, 13, 13, 14, 16) sts*
Next row (RS): Knit.
Cast off rem sts.

SLEEVES (pullover and cardigan)
Using smaller needles and Long-Tail Method, cast on 42 (44, 46, 50, 52, 54, 56, 58, 60) sts.
Row 1 (WS): P1, [k1, p1] to last st, p1.
Row 2 (RS): K2, [p1, k1] to end.
Rep rows 1-2 until piece measures 5cm / 2" from cast-on edge, ending with a WS row.

Change to larger needles.
Next row (RS): K12 (13, 14, 16, 17, 18, 19, 20, 21) sts, PM, work row 1 of Cable patt B over next 18 sts, PM, knit to end.
Next row (WS): Purl.

Standard length ONLY
Work 6 (4, 4, 4, 4, 2, 2, 2, 2) rows even in patt established by last 2 rows, working next row of patt between markers each time.

Inc row (RS): K2, RLI, k to marker, SM, work Cable patt B, SM, knit to last 2 sts, LLI, k2. *2 sts inc*
Rep Inc row every 8th (6th, 6th, 6th, 6th, 4th, 4th, 4th, 4th) row a further 9 (11, 12, 12, 13, 15, 18, 19, 19) times, maintaining established patt between markers. *62 (68, 72, 76, 80, 86, 94, 98, 100) sts*
Work even in patt until sleeve measures 44.5cm / 17½" ending with a WS row.

Tall length ONLY

Work 8 (6, 6, 6, 6, 6, 4, 4, 4) rows even in patt established by last 2 rows, working next row of patt between markers each time.
Inc row (RS): K2, RLI, knit to marker, SM, work Cable patt B, SM, knit to last 2 sts, LLI, k2. *2 sts inc*
Rep Inc row every 10th (8th, 8th, 8th, 8th, 8th, 6th, 6th, 6th) row a further 5 (11, 12, 12, 9, 3, 13, 11, 11) times, then every 8th (0, 0, 0, 6th, 6th, 4th, 4th, 4th) row a further 4 (0, 0, 0, 4, 12, 5, 8, 8) times. *62 (68, 72, 76, 80, 86, 94, 98, 100) sts*
Work even in patt until sleeve measures 51cm / 20", ending with a WS row.

BOTH lengths:
Shape Sleeve Cap
Cast off 5 (6, 6, 8, 8, 9, 9, 10, 10) sts at beg of next 2 rows. *52 (56, 60, 60, 64, 68, 76, 78, 80) sts*

Size 4 ONLY:
Work 2 rows even in patt.

ALL Sizes again:
Dec row (RS): K1, k2tog, patt to last 3 sts, ssk, k1. *2 sts dec*
Rep Dec row every 4th row a further 2 (2, 2, 3, 3, 4, 4, 5, 5) times, then work Dec row every RS row 5 (5, 7, 5, 8, 9, 8, 8, 8) times, maintaining established patt between markers. *36 (40, 40, 42, 40, 40, 50, 50, 52) sts*

Next row (WS): P1, ssp, patt to last 3 sts, p2tog, p1. *2 sts dec*
Next row (RS): K1, k2tog, patt to last 3 sts, ssk, k1. *2 sts dec*
Rep last 2 rows a further 1 (2, 2, 3, 2, 2, 4, 4, 5) time(s). *28 (28, 28, 26, 28, 28, 30, 30, 28) sts*
Cast off 5 sts at beg of next 4 rows.
Cast off rem 8 (8, 8, 6, 8, 8, 10, 10, 8) sts.

FINISHING
Block pieces to measurements. Sew shoulder seams. Set sleeves into armholes and sew sleeve seams and side seams using mattress stitch for a seamless finish.

Pullover ONLY:
Neck edging
With smaller circular needle, beg at top of left shoulder, pick up and knit 18 sts down left front neck edge, 15 (15, 15, 17, 17, 17, 17, 19, 19) sts into cast-off sts of front neck, 18 sts up right front neck edge, and 35 (35, 35, 37, 37, 37, 37, 39, 39) sts along back neck edge.
86 (86, 86, 90, 90, 90, 90, 94, 94) sts
PM and join to work in the round. Work in 1x1 Rib for 2.5cm / 1".
Cast off all sts. Weave in ends and block to schematic measurements.

Cardigan ONLY:
Left Button Band:
With RS facing and smaller circular needle, beg at top Left Front edge, pick up and knit 81 (85, 91, 97, 99, 105, 111, 115, 119) sts for standard length, or 91 (95, 99, 105, 109, 115, 119, 123, 127) sts for Tall version (approx 3 sts for every 4 rows).

Row 1 (WS): P2, [k1, p1] to last 3 sts, k1, p2.
Row 2 (RS): K2, [p1, k1] to last 3 sts, p1, k2.
Rep rows 1-2 rows a further 2 times, and then work row 1 only once more.
Cast off in patt.

Right Button Band:
With RS facing and smaller needle, beg at lower edge of bottom Right Front, pick up 81 (85, 91, 97, 99, 105, 111, 115, 119) sts for the standard length, or 91 (95, 99, 105, 109, 115, 119, 123, 127) for Tall version (approx 3 sts for every 4 rows).
Row 1 (WS): P2, [k1, p1] to last 3 sts, k1, p2.
Row 2 (RS): K2, [p1, k1] to last 3 sts, p1, k2.
Rep row 1 once more.

With RS facing, mark placement of 7 buttons for the Standard version and 8 buttons for the Tall version on needle with removable stitch markers, placing first marker 4 sts in from beginning of row and last marker 3 sts in from end of row.

Working from the right to left, place rem 5 (6) markers evenly spaced between, placing markers after a knit stitch.

Buttonhole row (RS): [Work in established rib patt to marker, remove marker, yo, k2tog] 7 (8) times, patt to end.

Rep rows 1 and 2 once more. Cast off in patt.

Neck Edging

With smaller circular needle, beg at open right neck edge, pick up and knit 6 sts along side edge of right button band, 8 (8, 8, 9, 9, 9, 9, 10, 10) sts into bind off sts of right front neck, 18 sts up right front neck edge, 35 (35, 35, 37, 37, 37, 37, 39, 39) sts along back neck edge, 18 sts down left front neck edge, 8 (8, 8, 9, 9, 9, 9, 10, 10) sts into bind off sts of left front neck and knit 6 sts along side edge of left button band. *99 (99, 99, 103, 103, 103, 103, 107, 107) sts*

For Crew Neck Edging ONLY:

Row 1 (WS): Sl1 pwise wyif, [p1, k1] to last 2 sts, p2.

Row 2 (RS): Sl1 pwise wyib, [k1, p1] to last 2 sts, k2.

Rep row 1 once more.

Buttonhole row (RS): Sl1 pwise wyib, k1, yo, k2tog, patt to end.

Rep rows 1-2 once more. Cast off in patt.

For Long Collar Edging ONLY:

Row 1 (WS): Sl1 pwise wyib, k2, [p1, k1] to last 4 sts, p2, k3.

Row 2 (RS): Sl1 pwise wyif, p2, [k1, p1] to last 4 sts, k1, p3.

Rep rows 1-2 until collar measures 9cm / 3½". Cast off in patt.

Sew buttons on to Left button band to correspond with buttonholes. Weave in all ends and block to schematic measurements.

Cable Pattern A

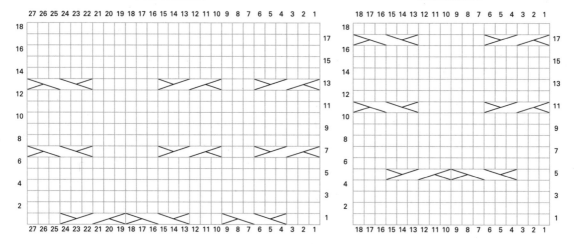

Cable Pattern B

Cable Pattern C

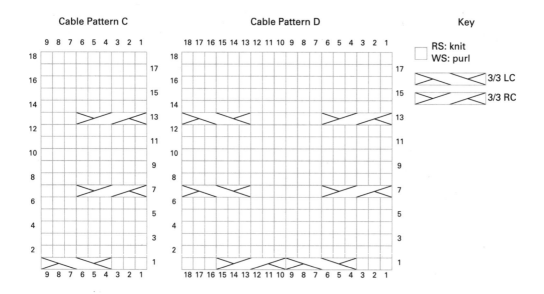

Cable Pattern D

Key

RS: knit	
WS: purl	
	3/3 LC
	3/3 RC

Schematic Measurements

a. Back width (pullover and cardigan): 43 (48.5, 53.5, 58.5, 63.5, 68.5, 73.5, 79, 84)cm / 17 (19, 21, 23, 25, 27, 29, 31, 33)"

b. Front width (cardigan, including buttonband): 21 (24, 26, 29, 31, 34.5, 36, 39.5, 41.5)cm / 8¼ (9½, 10¼, 11½, 12¼, 13½,14¼, 15½,16¼)"

c. Hem to underarm (standard length): 38 (39.5, 40.5, 42, 43, 44.5, 45, 47, 48.5)cm / 15 (15½, 16, 16½, 17, 17½, 18, 18½, 19)"

Hem to underarm (tall length): 43 (44.5, 45, 47, 48.5, 49.5, 51, 52, 53.5)cm / 17 (17½, 18, 18½,19, 19½, 20, 20½, 21)"

d. Armhole depth: 18 (19, 20.5, 23, 24, 25.5, 27, 28, 29.5)cm / 7 (7½, 8, 9, 9½, 10, 10½, 11, 11½)"

e. Back neck width: 16 (16, 16, 17, 17, 17, 17, 18, 18)cm / 6¼ (6¼, 6¼, 6¾, 6¾, 6¾, 6¾, 7, 7)"

f. Upper arm circumference: 32.5 (36, 38, 40.5, 42.5, 46, 50.5, 53, 54)cm / 12¾ (14, 15, 16, 16¾, 18, 20, 20¾, 21¼)"

g. Sleeve length (standard): 44.5cm / 17½"
Sleeve length (tall): 51cm / 20"

KORDY

In the early 60s, it was reported by Polish astronomer Kazimierz Kordylewski that there were two dust clouds orbiting the Earth. There was much speculation as to whether they could actually be moons, or if they even existed at all. In recent years, it has been confirmed that these clouds do exist. They are known as Kordylewski clouds. It would've been pretty neat if Earth had two more (twin) moons. Dust clouds seem less cool.

Colourwork yoke sweaters are a fun opportunity to play around and experiment with colour. This design's variation relies on colour to modify the look of the design. The sweater can feel very different when knit in bright contrasting colours, compared to working with more neutral subdued hues. To make this yoke really pop, choose colours that have high contrast. Contrast doesn't necessarily mean light and dark, but could be a contrast of bright versus pale. A helpful tip is to simply look at a colour wheel and choose complementary hues (colours that sit opposite each other on the wheel).

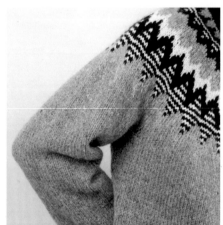

A more subdued and soft colour combo can also have an equally pleasing effect. Choose colours within the same family, and which are at a similar chromatic level. Chroma refers to the intensity of a colour. How to find it? Look at your colours together and squint. If they are at a similar chromatic level, they will blend together! Need help choosing your colours? See the swatches at the end of the pattern for some colour inspiration!

KORDY

Sizes: 1 (2, 3, 4, 5, 6, 7, 8, 9)
Finished chest (fullest point) circumference:
86 (96.5, 106.5, 117, 127, 137, 147, 157.5, 167.5)
cm / 34 (38, 42, 46, 50, 54, 58, 62, 66)" – to be
worn with approx 10cm / 4" positive ease

Paul's height is 175cm / 5'9", with a chest
(fullest point) circumference of 91.5cm / 36",
and is shown wearing the tall version in size
4 on page 74.

Kiyomi's height is 155cm / 5'1", with a chest
(fullest point) circumference of 84cm / 33",
and is shown wearing the standard version
in size 2 on page 75 and size 4 on page 73.

Sachiko's height is 157.5cm / 5'2", with a chest
(fullest point) circumference of 76cm / 30",
and is shown wearing the standard version
in size 2 on page 73.

Yarn: Peace Fleece Worsted (worsted-weight;
75% Navajo Rambouillet & domestic fine wool,
25% mohair; 190m / 200yds per 100g skein)

Shades Shown:
Standard length (grey/brown)
Yarn A: Negotiation Grey; 3 (4, 4, 5, 5, 5, 6, 6, 7)
skeins
Yarn B: Chestnut; 1 skein
Yarn C: Palomino; 1 skein
Yarn D: Antarctic White; 1 skein

Tall length (purple/black)
Yarn A: Latvian Lavender; 4 (4, 5, 5, 6, 6, 6, 6, 7)
skeins
Yarn B: Baku Black; 1 skein
Yarn C: Wild Mustard; 1 skein
Yarn D: Antarctic White; 1 skein

OR
Yarn A: 565 (640, 710, 785, 860, 925, 995, 1080,
1155)m / 595 (675, 745, 825, 900, 975, 1050,
1140, 1215) yds

For Tall version, an additional: 80 (110, 90, 115,
95, 80, 60, 30, 5)m / 87 (120, 98, 125, 103, 87,
65, 32, 6)yds of worsted-weight yarn.
Yarn B: 80 (85, 100, 110, 120, 120, 140, 160, 170)
m / 90 (95, 110, 120, 130, 130, 150, 175, 185)yds

Yarn C: 80 (85, 100, 110, 120, 120, 140, 160, 170)
m / 90 (95, 110, 120, 130, 130, 150, 175, 185)yds
Yarn D: 50 (60, 70, 80, 90, 100, 110, 120, 130)m
/ 55 (65, 75, 90, 100, 110, 120, 130, 140)yds

**For Contrast Neckband and Cuffs (optional),
an additional:**
Yarn B: 70 (75, 80, 85, 85, 90, 90, 95, 95)m /
75 (80, 85, 90, 90, 95, 100, 105, 105) yds
Yarn D: 15 (15, 15, 15, 25, 25, 25, 25, 25)m /
20 (20, 20, 20, 30, 30, 30, 30, 30) yds

Gauge: 16 sts & 24 rows = 10cm / 4" over
St st on 5mm needles, after blocking.

18 sts & 24 rows = 10cm / 4" over 2x2 Rib
on 4.5mm needles, after blocking.

Needles: 5mm / US 8 circular needle, 60cm
/ 24" length for yoke, 80cm / 32" length (or
longer for larger sizes) for body AND needles
suitable for working small circumferences in
the round
4.5mm / US 7 circular needle, 40cm / 16"
length AND needles suitable for working
small circumferences in the round

*Always use a needle size that will result in
the correct gauge after blocking.*

Notions: 2 stitch markers, tapestry needle

Notes: Pullover is worked from the top
down almost exclusively in the round.
The neckband is worked first, followed by
the colourwork yoke. After the colourwork
section is completed, the back yoke is
shaped by a small gusset section that is
worked back and forth for a better fit. The
body and sleeves are then divided and
worked separately in the round.

When working the stranded colourwork,
keep floats in the back loose to maintain
fabric elasticity. This design doesn't have
too many long floats, however when there
is a section of 5 stitches or more, it is
recommended to twist yarns together in
the back of work to help maintain gauge
and elasticity.

PATTERN BEGINS
Neck
Using smaller circular needle, yarn A (or B for contrasting neckband), and the Long-Tail Method, cast on 76 (76, 80, 84, 88, 92, 96, 100, 100) sts. Join for working in the round being careful not to twist. PM to indicate beg of round.

Work in 2x2 Rib until neck measures 5cm / 2" from cast-on edge.

Yoke
Change to larger circular needle for the next round, changing to longer needle when necessary as yoke increases.

Inc round: [K38, (9, 5, 4, 4, 4, 4, 4, 2), M1] 2 (4, 16, 6, 10, 8, 6, 4, 14) times, [k0 (10, 0, 5, 3, 3, 3, 3, 3), M1] 0 (4, 0, 12, 16, 20, 24, 28, 24) times. *78 (84, 96, 102, 114, 120, 126, 132, 138) sts*

Next round: Joining colours as necessary, work row 1 of Chart 26 (28, 32, 34, 38, 40, 42, 44, 46) times to end.
Continue through row 54 of Chart, skipping rows for your size as shown in chart. *208 (224, 256, 272, 304, 320, 336, 352, 368) sts*

Work even in St st with yarn A for 2 (2, 4, 4, 6, 6, 8, 10, 12) rounds, or until yoke fits comfortably to underarm when tried on (to try on, place all sts on a very long piece of waste yarn).

Back Gusset
Next round: K64 (68, 78, 82, 92, 98, 104, 110, 116) sts for back, then place rem sts of round on 3 separate pieces of waste yarn in the following order: 40 (44, 50, 54, 60, 62, 64, 66, 68) sts for right sleeve, 64 (68, 78, 82, 92, 98, 104, 110, 116) sts for front, and 40 (44, 50, 54, 60, 62, 64, 66, 68) sts for left sleeve.
Working back and forth in St st over back sts only, work 7 rows, ending with a WS row.

Divide for Body and Sleeves
Next round (RS): K64 (68, 78, 82, 92, 98, 104, 110, 116) sts for back, using the Backwards-Loop Method, cast on 4 (8, 6, 10, 8, 10, 12, 14, 16) sts for right underarm, skip held sts for right sleeve, transfer next 64 (68, 78, 82, 92, 98, 104, 110, 116) sts for front onto

needle and knit across these sts, skip held sts for left sleeve, using the Backwards-Loop Method, cast on 4 (8, 6, 10, 8, 10, 12, 14, 16) sts for left underarm placing a marker for beg of round in the centre of cast-on sts, and rejoin work in round. Knit to beg of round marker. *136 (152, 168, 184, 200, 216, 232, 248, 264) sts*

Work even in St st in the round until body measures 29cm / 11½" from underarm for standard length or 34cm / 13½" for tall length, or until body measures 6cm / 2½" less than finished desired length.

Change to smaller circular needle and work in 2x2 Rib until hem measures 6cm / 2½". Cast off loosely in pattern.

RIGHT SLEEVE
Using larger needle suitable for working small circumferences, return 40 (44, 50, 54, 60, 62, 64, 66, 68) sts for right sleeve back onto needle.

Join yarn A at centre of underarm, pick up and knit 2 (4, 3, 5, 4, 5, 6, 7, 8) sts from cast-on, pick up and knit 6 sts up side of back gusset, knit across 40 (44, 50, 54, 60, 62, 64, 66, 68) sleeve sts, pick up and knit 1 st in the gap between sleeve and underarm, then pick up and knit 2 (4, 3, 5, 4, 5, 6, 7, 8) sts from cast-on sts. PM to indicate beg of round. *51 (59, 63, 71, 75, 79, 83, 87, 91) sts*

Next round: K to last 3 (5, 4, 6, 5, 6, 7, 8, 9) sts, ssk, k to end. *50 (58, 62, 70, 74, 78, 82, 86, 90) sts*

Work *Standard Sleeve* or *Tall Sleeve* shaping instructions.

Standard Sleeve ONLY
Work 11 (9, 9, 7, 5, 5, 5, 4, 3) rounds even in St st.
Dec round: K1, k2tog, k to last 3 sts, ssk, k1.
2 sts dec
Rep Dec round every following 12th (10th, 10th, 8th, 6th, 6th, 6th, 5th, 4th) round a further 6 (8, 8, 10, 12, 14, 14, 16, 18) times.
36 (40, 44, 48, 48, 48, 52, 52, 52) sts

If necessary, work even in St st until sleeve measures 40.5cm / 16" from underarm, or until sleeve measures 5cm / 2" less than finished desired length.

Tall Sleeve ONLY
Work 14 (11, 11, 7, 7, 6, 6, 5, 5) rnds even in St st.
Dec round: K1, k2tog, knit to last 3 sts, ssk, k1. *2 sts dec*
Rep dec round every following 15th (12th, 12th, 9th, 8th, 7th, 7th, 6th, 5th) round a further 6 (8, 8, 10, 12, 14, 14, 16, 18) times. *36 (40, 44, 48, 48, 48, 52, 52, 52) sts*

If necessary, work even in St st until sleeve measures 48cm / 19" from underarm, or until sleeve measures 5cm / 2" less than finished desired length.

BOTH versions
Change to smaller needle.
Work *Plain Cuffs* or *Striped Contrasting Cuffs*.

Plain Cuffs
Work in 2x2 Rib until cuff measures 5cm / 2". Cast off loosely in pattern.
Striped Contrasting Cuffs
Break yarn A and join yarn B and D. Do not break yarns between colour changes.
Round 1: With yarn B, knit.
Round 2: With yarn B, work 1x1 Rib.
Round 3: With yarn D, work 1x1 Rib.
Rounds 4-5: With yarn B, work 1x1 Rib.
Rep rounds 3-5 a further 3 times. Break yarn D and cast off loosely in pattern with yarn B.

LEFT SLEEVE
Using larger needle suitable for working small circumferences, return 40 (44, 50, 54, 60, 62, 64, 66, 68) sts for left sleeve back onto needle. Join yarn A at centre of underarm, and pick up and knit 2 (4, 3, 5, 4, 5, 6, 7, 8) sts from cast-on sts, pick up and knit 1 st in gap between underarm and sleeve, knit across 40 (44, 50, 54, 60, 62, 64, 66, 68) sleeve sts, pick up and knit 6 sts down side of back gusset, pick up and knit 2 (4, 3, 5, 4, 5, 6, 7, 8) sts from cast-on sts. PM to indicate beg of round. *51 (59, 63, 71, 75, 79, 83, 87, 91) sts*

Next round: K1 (3, 2, 4, 3, 4, 5, 6, 7), k2tog, k to end. *50 (58, 62, 70, 74, 78, 82, 86, 90) sts*

Work *Standard Sleeve* or *Tall Sleeve* shaping instructions as for right sleeve.

Change to smaller needle.

Work *Plain Cuffs* or *Striped Contrasting Cuffs* as for right sleeve.

FINISHING
Weave in ends and block to measurements.

Key

☐ knit

⅂ M1

▨ Yarn A

■ Yarn B

▥ Yarn C

☐ Yarn D

Chart

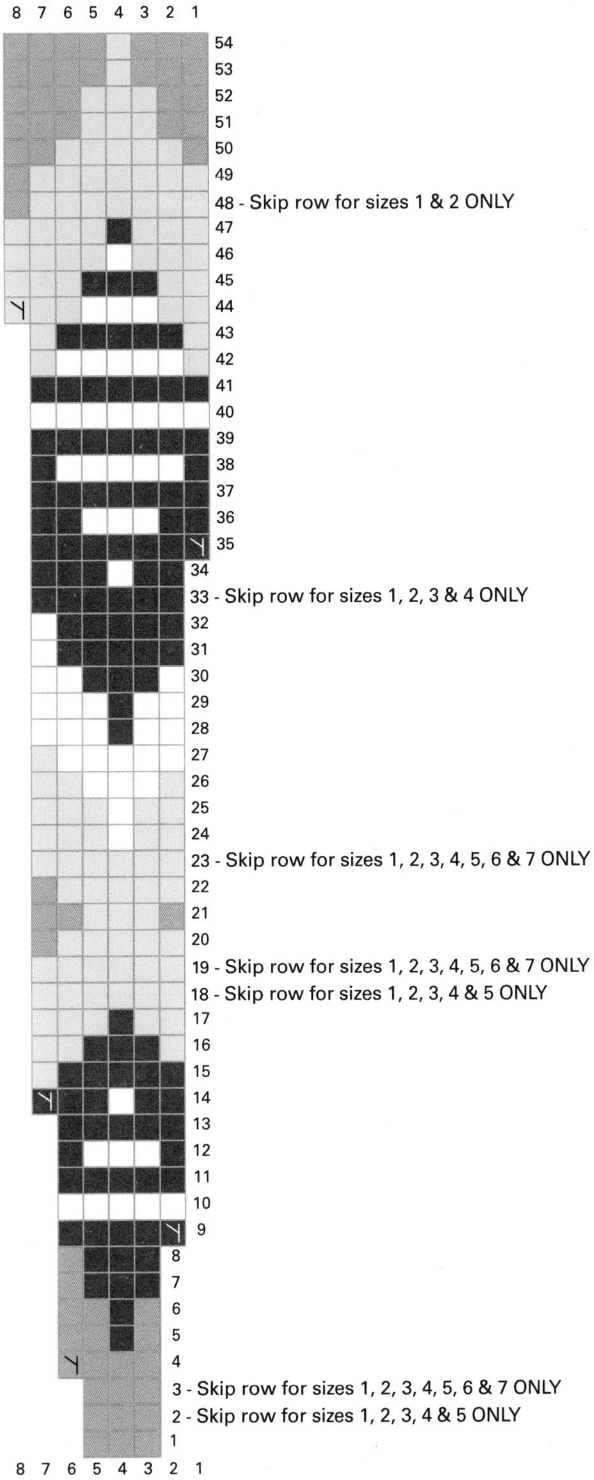

8 7 6 5 4 3 2 1

54
53
52
51
50
49
48 - Skip row for sizes 1 & 2 ONLY
47
46
45
44
43
42
41
40
39
38
37
36
35
34
33 - Skip row for sizes 1, 2, 3 & 4 ONLY
32
31
30
29
28
27
26
25
24
23 - Skip row for sizes 1, 2, 3, 4, 5, 6 & 7 ONLY
22
21
20
19 - Skip row for sizes 1, 2, 3, 4, 5, 6 & 7 ONLY
18 - Skip row for sizes 1, 2, 3, 4 & 5 ONLY
17
16
15
14
13
12
11
10
9
8
7
6
5
4
3 - Skip row for sizes 1, 2, 3, 4, 5, 6 & 7 ONLY
2 - Skip row for sizes 1, 2, 3, 4 & 5 ONLY
1

8 7 6 5 4 3 2 1

Schematic Measurements

a. Finished chest (fullest point) circumference:
86 (96.5, 106.5, 117, 127, 137, 147, 157.5, 167.5)
cm / 34 (38, 42, 46, 50, 54, 58, 62, 66)"
b. Length to underarm, standard: 35.5cm / 14"
Length to underarm, tall: 40.5cm / 16"
c. Upper arm circumference: 32 (37, 39.5, 44.5,
47, 49.5, 52, 54.5, 57)cm / 12½ (14½, 15½,
17½, 18½, 19½, 20½, 21½, 22½)"
d. Sleeve length, standard: 46cm / 18"
Sleeve length, tall: 53.5cm / 21"
e. Yoke depth: 21 (21, 22.5, 22.5, 24, 24.5, 25.5,
27.5, 28.5)cm / 8¼ (8¼, 8¾, 8¾, 9¼, 9½, 10,
10¾, 11)"
f. Neck opening: 43 (43, 45, 47.5, 49.5, 52, 54,
56.5, 56.5)cm / 16¾ (16¾, 17¾, 18½, 19½,
20½, 21¼, 22¼, 22¼)"

Kordy Swatches

Colour can really change how something looks and feels, and says a lot about the person who chose them. On this page we've provided some additional colour combos for the *Kordy* yoke sweater to help get your creativity flowing!

Knit in Peace Fleece Worsted from left to right:

Yarn A: Tundra
Yarn B: Kamchatka Sea Moss
Yarn C: Mourning Dove
Yarn D: Antarctic White

Yarn A: Lily Pad
Yarn B: Bonnie Blue Cap
Yarn C: Baltic Blue
Yarn D: Antarctic White

Yarn A: Sheplova Mushroom
Yarn B: Brownie
Yarn C: Negotiation Grey
Yarn D: Antarctic White

Yarn A: Zarya Fog
Yarn B: Antarctic White
Yarn C: Palomino
Yarn D: Fathers Grey

LEWSKY

I love hoods, whereas Sachiko isn't a huge fan, so the decision to make this hood a separate piece was pretty straightforward. It's a nice addition to the *Kordy* yoke sweater, making it much more suitable as an outdoor garment. The hood also has the option to add a face shield: an extra layer on the inside that you can wear scrunched around the neck or pulled up over your nose. It makes the hood super warm (like super duper warm!), and might only be suitable for the coldest days. ~ *Kiyomi*

Yes, it's true. In the past, I haven't been much of a hood fan. Maybe it's because I've always had long hair and find layering jackets on top awkward. We argued a bit on this one. I thought a knitted hood on a yoke sweater would be heavy and pull the neck back in an uncomfortable way. Even though I've come around to the idea of a hooded sweater, I was really pleased with the decision to make the hood a separate piece. It's a handy thing to have in any colder climate and it features a few fun and unexpected techniques to keep the knitting interesting. ~ *Sachiko*

Additional Variation Suggestion
A fun modification you could try would
be to use a lighter yarn to make a more
airy face shield or perhaps try knitting
it in a different fibre, like mohair!

1 (2, 3)

C.... nference: 61 (66, 71)cm / 24 (26, 28)"
– to be worn with approx 12-18cm / 5-7"
positive ease

Greg and Paul are shown wearing size 3
on pages 82, 83, 84, 85 and 89.

Kiyomi is shown wearing size 2 with
face shield on pages 84 and 85.

Yarn: Peace Fleece Worsted (worsted-weight;
75% Navajo Rambouillet & domestic fine
wool, 25% mohair; 190m / 200yds per 100g
skein)

Shades Shown:
Yarn A: Baku Black; 2 skeins
Yarn B: Wild Mustard; 1 skein

Version with face shield:
Yarn A: Negotiation Grey
Yarn B: Chestnut

OR
Yarn A: approx. 275 (300, 350)m / 300 (325,
385)yds of worsted-weight yarn
Yarn B: approx. 9m / 10yds for drawcord
PLUS an additional 145 (155, 170)m / 160
(170, 185)yds of worsted-weight yarn for
Face Shield

Gauge: 16 sts & 24 rows = 10cm / 4" over St
st on 5mm needles, after blocking.

32 sts & 52 rows = 10cm / 4" over double knit
pattern on 3.75mm needles, after blocking.

Needles & hooks: 5mm / US 8 circular
needle, 60cm / 24" length
4.5mm / US 7 circular needle, 60cm / 24"
length, and a spare circular needle
3.75mm / US 5 circular needle, 40cm / 16"
length, and a spare circular needle
Crochet hook for provisional cast-on

*Always use a needle size that will result in
the correct gauge after blocking.*

Notions: 2 stitch markers, waste yarn for
provisional cast-on, stitch holders or waste
yarn, cable needle, tapestry needle, large
safety pin

Notes: Hood is worked from the bottom
up from a folded hem. Drawcord casing is
picked up and knit around the face opening
and worked as a double knit tube that is
grafted closed at the end. An optional face
shield can be added by picking up and
knitting sts from the folded hem. To choose
pattern size, measure head circumference
and add 12-18cm / 5-7" to that measurement.
Choose pattern finished circumference size
that will give you the closest finished size.

PATTERN BEGINS
Hem
Using 4.5mm circular needle, crochet hook,
and waste yarn, cast on 96 (104, 112) sts
using the Crochet Provisional Cast-On
Method.
Join yarn A and knit one row. Join for
working in the round being careful not to
twist. PM to indicate beg of round.

Work 16 rounds even in St st.

Carefully remove waste yarn from
provisional cast-on and place these sts onto
spare circular needle. *96 (104, 112) sts*

Fold work up to inside so that the WS of
fabric is together and needles are parallel,
with the spare needle at the back.
Using working (front) needle, insert RH
needle tip into the first st on the front
(working) needle then the first stitch on the
spare (back) needle. Knit these two sts
together and slip both sts from LH needles.
Continue in this manner until all 96 (104, 112)
sts have been worked and spare needle is
removed.

Neck
Change to 5mm circular needle and work in
St st in the round until piece measures 20cm
/ 8" from folded bottom edge, ending last
round 8 sts before beg of round.

Place next 16 sts on holder or waste yarn removing marker as you pass it, turn. You will now be working back and forth in St st. *80 (88, 96) sts*

Shape Hood Face Opening
Row 1 (WS): Purl.

Row 2 (RS)(dec): K1, k2tog, k to last 3 sts, ssk, k1. *2 sts dec*
Rep rows 1-2 a further 3 (5, 7) times. *72 (76, 80) sts*

Work even back and forth in St st until piece measures 15 (16.5, 18)cm / 6 (6½, 7)" from the sts 16 sts previously placed on hold, ending with a WS row. Place a marker after 36 (38, 40) sts at centre back.

Shape Top of Hood
Row 1 (RS)(dec): Knit to 10 sts before marker, k2tog, k to marker, SM, k8, ssk, k to end. *2 sts dec*
Row 2 (WS): Purl.
Rep rows 1-2 a further 3 times. *64 (68, 72) sts*

Next row (RS): K to back marker, remove marker, k8, ssk, turn. *1 st dec*

Next row (WS): P17, p2tog, turn. *1 st dec*
Next row (RS): K17, ssk, turn. *1 st dec*
Rep last two rows, working over centre sts only until 18 sts rem. Break yarn and place rem sts on holder or waste yarn.

Drawcord Casing (edging around face opening)
Return the 16 sts on holder or waste yarn at base of face opening back onto 3.75mm circular needle and join yarn A.

Next row (RS): K1, k2tog, k10, ssk, k1, PM, pick up and knit 28 (30, 32) sts up right edge of face opening, PM, place 18 sts at top of face opening onto LH needle, k1, k2tog, k12, ssk, k1, pick up and knit 28 (30, 32) sts down left edge of face opening, PM to indicate beg of round. *86 (90, 94) sts*

Set-up round: [K1, yo] to marker, SM, [k1, yo] to end. *172 (180, 188) sts*
Round 1: [K1, sl1 pwise wyif] to end, slipping marker as you pass it.
Round 2: [Sl1 pwise wyib, p1] to end, slipping marker as you pass it.
Rounds 3-4: Rep rounds 1-2 once more.
Round 5: [K1, sl1 pwise wyif] to marker, SM, k1, sl1 pwise wyif, yo, slip next st onto cable needle pwise and hold in front, sl1 pwise wyif, slip st on cable needle back to LH needle and k2tog, sl1 pwise wyif, [k1, sl1 pwise wyif] to last 4 sts, sl1 pwise, slip next st pwise to cable needle and hold in back, slip st on RH needle back to LH needle and ssk, slip st on cable needle to RH needle wyif, yo, sl1 pwise wyif.
Round 6: Rep round 2.
Rounds 7-10: Rep rounds 1-2 twice more.

Next round: Slipping each st pwise, slip the knit sts onto the working needle and the purl sts onto a spare circular needle, held at the back, removing marker as you pass it (leave beg of round marker in place). *86 (90, 94) sts on each needle*

Break yarn, leaving a tail that is approx 4 times the circumference of face opening. Thread tail onto a tapestry needle and graft front sts together with back sts.

Face Shield (optional)
Turn hood to WS.

With hem facing downwards, using 4.5mm circular needle and yarn B, pick up and knit 1 st into each "smile" bump just above the turned hem until there are 96 (104, 112) sts on needle. PM to indicate beg of round.

Work in 2x2 Rib in the round until piece measures 23cm / 9" from turned hem. Cast off loosely in pattern.

FINISHING
Drawcord

With yarn B, cut 3 strands of approx 2.75m / 3yds long each. Holding strands together, fold in half, and tie an overhand knot approx 2.5cm / 1" down from folded end to form a loop. Secure this loop onto something (top of chair, drawer handle, under a heavy pile of books, etc.), divide strands into two sections of 3 strands each. Holding both sections near the cut ends, twist sections clockwise until each section is very tightly twisted (approx 160 twists). Using an overhand knot, fasten ends together, and let strand go. The strand should naturally twist on itself to form a nice evenly spiralled cord! Trim ends.

Weave in ends and block to measurements. Draw cord through casing using a large safety pin, by going up through either yarn over hole and around the face opening. The tube is closed at the bottom left side.

Schematic Measurements

a. **Circumference:** 61 (66, 71)cm / 24 (26, 28)"
b. **Full Length (excluding face shield):** 38 (39, 40.5)cm / 15 (15½, 16)"
c. **Neck Length:** 20cm / 8"
d: **Face Opening:** 39.5 (40.5, 42)cm / 15½ (16, 16½)"
e. **Face Shield Length:** 23cm / 9"

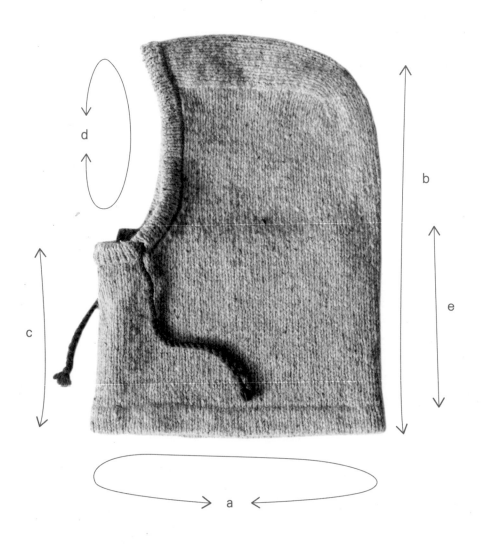

ESP is a toque. I've always enjoyed the word toque. Maybe because it's a term somewhat inherent to Canadian dialects of English and French, or that no one can agree on the spelling (Tuque? Touque?). Mostly I just prefer it to the word beanie, which sounds to me like a word you would use to complain about eating something with too many beans in it. This toque features a fun-to-knit colourwork motif that's geometric and stripey. You can choose to knit it with a short brim or a longer folded-up brim. The other pattern variation we used was to put the colourwork pattern on the *Zener* socks. Both patterns also coordinate with the *Kordy* yoke sweater too. ~ *Kiyomi*

Ki had actually made a swatch for this design years ago, and it was pinned to a swatch board in her tiny Brooklyn sewing room. I was always drawn to it and, every time I visited, I would pull it down and bother her about finally doing something with it. If she didn't act fast, I threatened to use it for one of my own designs. As per Ki's usual habit of patience, she waited until the right idea came to mind and I'm glad she didn't rush it because I really love how this toque came out! Despite being a three-coloured toque, the colourwork is deceptively easy because you're never using more than two colours per round. ~ *Sachiko*

Not pronounced as 'esp', but E.S.P.! ESP stands for extrasensory perception: the ability to read someone's mind! Many believe that twins possess this power. Is it true? We think so.

Additional Variation Suggestion
Incorporating additional colours into
this design could be really neat. Play
around with the chart and see what
you come up with! Also try wearing
this toque inside out to show off the
cool stranding on the wrong side.

E S P

Sizes: 1 (2, 3)
Finished circumference: 46.5 (51, 55)cm /
18¼ (20, 21¾)" - to be worn with approx
2.5cm / 1" negative ease
Length, Short Brim: 23cm / 9"
Length, Folded Brim (unfolded): 28cm / 11"

Kiyomi is shown wearing the folded
brim version in size 1 on pages 90 and 91.

Sachiko is shown wearing the short
brim version in size 2 on pages 90 and 91.

Yarn: Akara Yarns Organic DK (DK-weight;
100% organic merino wool; 238m /
260yds per 115g skein)

Shades Shown:
Folded brim
Yarn A: Dark Like my Soul; 1 skein, or
 approx. 85 (90, 95)m / 90 (100, 105)yds
Yarn B: Lichen; 1 skein, or approx. 70
(75, 80)m / 75 (80, 90)yds
Yarn C: Snowy Owl; 1 skein, or approx.
55 (60, 65)m / 60 (65, 70)yds

Short brim
Yarn A: Incense; 1 skein, or approx. 60
(65, 70)m / 65 (70, 75)yds
Yarn B: Mochaccino; 1 skein, or approx.
70 (75, 80)m / 75 (80, 90)yds
Yarn C: Snowy Owl; 1 skein, or approx.
40 (45, 50)m / 45 (50, 55)yds

Gauge: 24 sts & 26 rows = 10cm / 4" over
colourwork pattern on 3.75mm needles,
after blocking.

27 sts & 34 rows = 10cm / 4" over 1x1 Rib
pattern on 3.25mm needles, unstretched
after blocking.

Needles: 3.25mm / US 3 straight needles (optional for Tubular Cast-On set up rows), and /
or circular needle, 40cm / 16" length
3.75mm / US 5 circular needle, 40cm / 16"
length AND needles suitable for working
small circumferences in the round
*Always use a needle size that will result
in the correct gauge after blocking.*

Notions: 1 stitch marker, tapestry needle,
pom pom maker (optional)

Notes: Hat is worked in one piece from
the brim up. The chart is worked using the
stranded colour work method. Keep floats
loose to maintain an elastic fabric. For floats
longer than 5 stitches, twist yarns together
on wrong side of work. Please check your
gauge by knitting a substantial swatch in
the charted pattern before beginning, as
stranded knitting can work up tighter
than you would normally knit.

PATTERN BEGINS
Brim
Using smaller straight or circular needles,
yarn A, and the Long-Tail Tubular Cast-On
method, cast on 110 (120, 130) sts.
Set-up row 1 (RS): [K1tbl, sl1 pwise wyif] to end.
Set-up row 2 (WS): [K1, sl1 pwise wyif] to end.
If using straight needles, change to smaller
circular needle.
Join for working in the round being careful
not to twist. PM to indicate beg of round.

Join yarn C. Do not break yarns between
colour changes.
Round 1: With yarn A, work in 1x1 Rib.
Round 2: With yarn C, work in 1x1 Rib.
Rounds 3-4: With yarn A, work in 1x1 Rib.
Rep rounds 2-4 until brim measures 5cm / 2"
from cast-on edge for a short brim, or 10cm /
4" from cast-on edge for a folded brim.

Body and Crown
Change to larger circular needle.

Next round: Join yarn B and work round
1 of Chart 11 (12, 13) times to end.
Continue through round 47 of Chart,
changing to needles suitable for working
small circumferences in the round when
necessary. *11 (12, 13) sts*
Next round: [K2tog] to last 1 (0, 1) sts, k1 (0,
1). *6 (6, 7) sts*

Break yarn leaving a long tail. Thread tail onto
tapestry needle and draw through rem sts.
Pull tight and fasten off on the inside of hat.

FINISHING

Weave in ends. Block flat to measurements in schematic. For version 2, fold brim up in half.

Speckled Pom-Pom (optional)

With a pom-pom maker and yarn A, make a pom-pom according to package instructions. When tying off strands, leave two 20cm/ 8" tails. Trim pom-pom. Using short pieces of yarn C, carefully thread pieces through pom-pom at random, and then trim down. Using tails, firmly attach pom-pom to centre of crown, fastening off on WS.

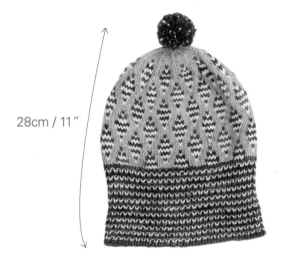

28cm / 11"

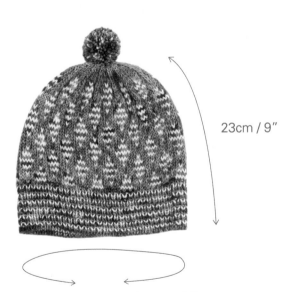

23cm / 9"

46.5 (51, 55)cm / 18¼ (20, 21¾)"

Chart

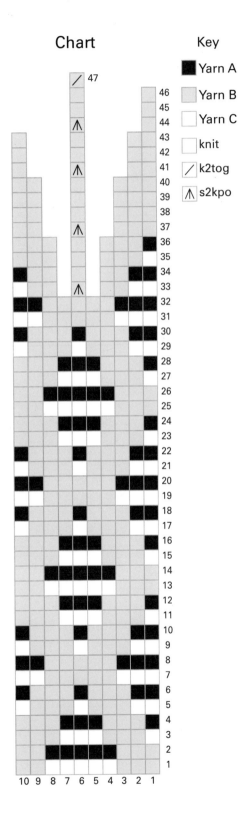

Key

- ■ Yarn A
- ▨ Yarn B
- □ Yarn C
- □ knit
- ╱ k2tog
- ⋀ s2kpo

E
S
P

TWIN TALK

Kiyomi talking about Sachiko

Chi (Sachiko) has always been my spokesperson. As a child, I was painfully shy to the point of sometimes being unable to utter a single word in the presence of others. Chi always jumped in for me and was my voice. I suppose this is why in adulthood I rely on her so heavily and find myself asking her advice on an idea or getting her approval for a design. Her opinion is the most important and sometimes even surpasses my own. I'm making myself sound very indecisive (not untrue), but it's really more that I appreciate and feel fortunate to always have her honest feedback.

Chi works in a completely different way, which for a person like me can seem almost reckless! She's very sure of herself, spontaneous, and doesn't require my assurances or input (much to my frustration). As soon as she gets an idea, she leaps into it with full force and a clear vision of the end result. She also works quickly, and her ideas seem to reach fruition almost overnight. However, based on the complexity and success of her output, I know she spends a lot of time planning her ideas, though I'm not sure when. I think it's probably in the middle of the night since she never seems to sleep. She's very technical, and has notebooks filled with funny drawings and long strings of numbers that look like gibberish, but she always seems to know and remember what they refer to.

Oftentimes, when she shares her ideas with me my first thought is: weird! She has a knack for choosing the last colours I would ever work with, and picks techniques and shaping I usually think are extreme. I get annoyed sometimes because I always want her to do things my way, but she is very stubborn! Then somehow, as the ideas unfold and materialise, they miraculously turn into something totally awesome that I end up loving.

Kiyomi (left) and Sachiko (right)

Her spontaneity adds a unique twist to her designs, which are full of imagination and force me to see things in a different way. I find myself super impressed every time. I think we are often each other's toughest critics. This is a good thing because it keeps us open to possibilities and new ideas. Twins can be so different, to the point of misunderstanding and disagreeing with each other, yet alike enough to know exactly what will appeal to the other, and what they actually need.

Chi surprises me constantly, and I'm always excited to see what she comes up with. Although we've shared a similar life path, hers has been a lot bumpier than mine, with many obstacles to overcome, so when I see her succeed, I feel super proud. Her success is mine, too!

Fun Chi Fact: She grades all her designs totally old school with paper and pencil, and completely without the use of spreadsheets!

Sachiko talking about Kiyomi

I find writing and talking about myself a difficult task, so I thought it would be an amusing idea to each write something about the other instead. It's pretty remarkable that after we had finished and read both texts, we found that we had written very similar things without discussing it beforehand! My sister Kiyomi is the 'younger' of the two of us, really just by chance, having been pulled out a few minutes after me during our cesarian birth. Despite my older and wiser twin stature, I consider Ki to be the more sensitive, logical and discerning twin, but not without whimsy or imagination. Ki has always had a strong sense of style, an adept understanding of colour theory, and an appreciation for all things practical and functional. She has always been a bit better at most creative endeavours than me (it must be her left-handedness), although it's not something I have ever felt competitive or jealous about.

Instead, I love to sit back and watch what will unfold; I always get super excited when she starts something new! As a somewhat impulsive person myself, I often find it a tad frustrating when we have to make a decision together. Ki really has to take her time to think about every aspect before committing to anything, regardless of how significant or trivial the decision may be. For example, when choosing a colour combination for a colourwork project; the decision could take weeks. Numerous charts in various colour combinations will be made - some with only minute differences. She will closely analyse how the colours work together in the project, as well as with her other handmade items, and then she will consider the longevity of the piece as a useful, enduring addition to her wardrobe. If something goes even slightly wrong, she won't hesitate to restart this process from scratch. I've witnessed her frog entire finished projects only a few moments after having bound off the final stitch just because she didn't like the way a set of decreases looked. When I tease her and call her a perfectionist, she calmly reminds me that there is nothing wrong with aiming to do your best work. I'm sure my spontaneous ways must aggravate her.

Despite the frustrations, the contrast in our practices has been really helpful as it pushes me not to settle with the first thing I think of, and to explore and keep questioning instead. I run every idea I have by her. I trust her judgement implicitly and know that she'll always be completely honest with me. Her level of meticulousness motivates me to try my best. She is the most creative and thoughtful person I know.

Fun Ki Fact: She is an expert sweater surgeon and is able to seamlessly graft in colour and stitch patterns.

ACKNOWLEDGEMENTS

Making this collection involved the minds, hands, and hearts of many people, and it feels literally impossible to express enough thanks in any meaningful way, but on this page we will try our best!

To the yarn dyers and yarn companies who provided us with your gorgeous yarn so that we could make our designs a reality.

To tech editors, Laura and Jemima. Thank you for your keen eyes!

To sample knitters, Emily, Lana and Stacey. Without your speedy needle skills, we would probably still be swimming in a pile of FOs (Finished Objects), so thank you from the bottom of our hearts.

To the test knitters, who so eagerly and generously offered their time to make sure our patterns are actually knittable!

To knitting friends, Amanda, Bree, Britt, Debirah, Emma, and Emily, who swooped in and answered our call for scrap yarn. Thank you for sharing your stashes!

To our models, Greg and Paul. Thank you for your patience with us!

Baby and Bochan (cats!), who oversaw quality control of all samples, and made sure each piece was nap-worthy.

To Oliver, for being a great photographer, and taking care of everything design related. Thanks for putting up with our constant 'knitpicking'.

To Mom, who read over our writing, provided buttons, sewed turtlenecks and helped with so many other things!

To Francesca, who came up with the most important detail of all: the book title! What would we do without your intelligence and penchant for research? We really don't know.

And finally, a huge thank you to the Pom Pom dream team, Lydia, Meghan, Amy, Francesca, Sophie, Belinda, Alice, Sofia, Noush, and Gayle. You made this book a reality and we are so grateful. Thank you.

Land Acknowledgement

The making of the majority of this book took place on the Ancestral and Traditional Territories of the Mississaugas of the Credit, the Haudenosaunee, the Anishnabeg, and the Wendat, known as Tkaronto, which has been home to many Indigenous, Métis, and Inuit people for millennia. The territory is covered by the Toronto Purchase Treaty 13 and is protected by the Dish With One Spoon Agreement.

When our ancestors travelled to Canada from Europe and Japan, they sought a place of opportunity and, upon arrival, opportunity is what they found here. Working within forestry, fishing, and farming, our predecessors benefitted from the resources this land provided and were able to build lives and security from which we, as descendants, now directly benefit. Our family has also been deeply affected by the generosity and stewardship of Canada's Indigenous people. Members of the Nisga'a First Nation worked alongside our family in British Columbia's fishing industry until after Canada declared war on Japan following the 1941 bombing of Pearl Harbour in the United States. Similar to the US government, the Canadian government then ordered the forced removal of Canadian citizens and residents of Japanese heritage along the Pacific Coast to harsh inland incarceration camps, banned them from returning to the coast, and impounded their property, supposedly as a 'temporary measure'. Our family complied with government demands, entrusting the government with the fishing boat of our great uncle Judo 'Jack' Tasaka, which he had built by hand. The Nyce and Gosnell families of the Nisga'a First Nation strongly protested the forced removal of Japanese Canadians. When the government later auctioned the property of Japanese Canadians to fund the prison camps, the Nyce family bought and protected the boat until our family was allowed to return. Japanese Canadians were required by the Canadian government to remain in inhumane living and working conditions or were sent to Japan, even after the war ended. Members of the Gosnell family successfully lobbied the Canadian government to lift the travel ban, allowing Japanese Canadians to finally return to the Pacific Coast in 1949. True to their word, the Nyce family returned the boat, helping our family to rebuild their livelihood. This great act of kindness is a symbol of kinship and holds profound importance for our family. We are eternally grateful to the Gosnell and Nyce families for standing up against injustice when many others did not.

Why put a land acknowledgement in a book? Because wherever you are reading this, whether that be North America or beyond, as settlers on any land, it is important to honour the Indigenous people past and present and acknowledge their rights to the land that they have looked after. What would we do without land and water? We must remember our privilege of being able to reside where we do and never forget the oppressive history of colonialism, our present participation in it, and how we must proceed in new ways and with new perspectives for the betterment of future generations.

ABBREVIATIONS

1x1 Rib (in the round): Round 1: [K1, p1] to end.
Rep round 1 for pattern.

2x2 Rib (in the round): Round 1: [K2, p2] to end.
Rep round 1 for pattern.

3/3 LC:	Slip 3 stitches to cable needle, hold at front, k3, k3 from cable needle.
3/3 RC:	Slip 3 stitches to cable needle, hold at back, k3, k3 from cable needle.
approx	approximately
beg	Beginning
dec	Decrease(d)
DPN(s)	Double-pointed needle(s)
foll	Follow(s)
inc	Increase(d)
k	Knit
k1b	Insert your right needle into the stitch directly below the stitch you are about to work, knitwise. Knit the stitch as normal, pulling the worked stitch and the stitch above off the needle together. The stitch above should unravel.
k1tbl	Knit 1 stitch through the back loop
k2tog	Knit 2 stitches together
kfb	Knit into the front and back of the next stitch
kwise	Knitwise
LH	Left hand
LLI	With left needle, pull up the stitch two rows below the stitch just knitted from back to front and leave it on the left needle. Knit this stitch.
LLIP	With left needle, pull up the stitch two rows below the stitch just purled from front to back and leave it on the left needle. Purl this stitch.
M1	(worked as a make 1 left)
M1L	Insert left needle, from front to back, under strand of yarn which runs between next stitch on left needle and last stitch on right needle, and knit this stitch through back loop.
M1R	Insert left needle, from back to front, under strand of yarn which runs between next stitch on left needle and last stitch on right needle, and knit this stitch through front loop.
p	Purl
patt	Pattern
p2tog	Purl 2 stitches together
pwise	Purlwise
PM	Place marker
rem	Remain(ing)
rep	Repeat(s)

RLI	With right needle, pull up the stitch one row below the first stitch on the left needle from back to front and place the stitch on the left needle. Knit this stitch and slip it off the needle.
RLIP	With right needle, pull up the purl stitch one row below the first stitch on the left needle and place the stitch on the left needle, so that the left leg of the stitch is in the back. Purl this stitch and slip it off the needle.
RH	Right hand
RS	Right side(s)
s2kpo	Slip 2 stitches together knitwise as if working a knit two together, k1, pass 2 slipped stitches over.
sl	Slip
SM	Slip marker
ssk	Slip 2 stitches knitwise one at a time, knit them together through the back loops
ssp	Slip 2 stitches knitwise one at a time, purl them together through the back loops
St st	Stockinette (stocking) stitch
st(s)	Stitches
WS	Wrong side(s)
wyib	With yarn held in back of work
wyif	With yarn held in front of work
yo	Yarn over needle and into working position
*	Repeat instructions from asterisk stated number of times
[ ]	Repeat instructions in brackets stated number of times

Ginsan Pocket Tutorial
kshandknitdesign.com/ginsanpockets

3-Needle Cast-Off
pompommag.com/three-needle-bind-off

Crochet Provisional Cast-On
pompommag.com/crochet-provisional-cast-on

Grafting
pompommag.com/grafting

I-Cord
pompommag.com/tutorials

Backwards Loop Cast-On
pompommag.com/tutorials

Long-Tail Cast-On
pompommag.com/tutorials

Long-Tail Tubular Cast-on
pompommag.com/tutorials

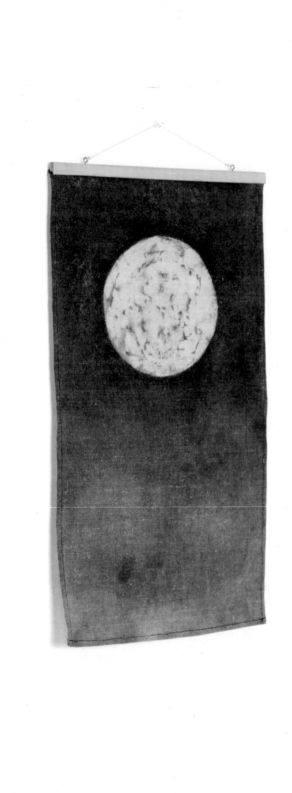